To all of You,
With many many thanks
for an amazing Fall 1907
in Norwich and beyond.
With much Love,
Wanaka's John and Jill.

CW00546925

HELLBENT
FOR THE POLE

HELLBENT
FOR THE POLE

Geoffrey Lee Martin

An insider's account of the
'race to the South Pole' 1957–58

RANDOM HOUSE
NEW ZEALAND

A catalogue record for this book is available from the National Library of New Zealand.

A RANDOM HOUSE BOOK
published by
Random House New Zealand
18 Poland Road, Glenfield, Auckland, New Zealand
www.randomhouse.co.nz

Random House International
Random House
20 Vauxhall Bridge Road
London, SW1V 2SA
United Kingdom

Random House Australia (Pty) Ltd
20 Alfred Street, Milsons Point, Sydney,
New South Wales 2061, Australia

Random House South Africa Pty Ltd
Isle of Houghton
Corner Boundary Road and Carse O'Gowrie
Houghton 2198, South Africa

Random House Publishers India Private Ltd
301 World Trade Tower, Hotel Intercontinental Grand Complex,
Barakhamba Lane, New Delhi 110 001, India

First published 2007

© 2007 Geoffrey Lee Martin

The moral rights of the author have been asserted

ISBN 978 1 86941 915 8

This book is copyright. Except for the purposes of fair reviewing no part of this publication may be reproduced or transmitted in any form or by any means, electronic or mechanical, including photocopying, recording or any information storage and retrieval system, without permission in writing from the publisher.

Cover and text design: Basil Williams
Photos on page 7 and back cover (author photo): Chris Gurr
Printed in China by Everbest Co Ltd

Contents

Acknowledgements

Firstly to my daughters and son who, far from becoming bored as I did after repeatedly seeing film-slide projections of these transparencies when they were young, kept nagging at me to dig them out from my files and `do something with them'.

Then to my friend Basil Williams, now living in Tucson, who, as a professional photo-journalist and illustrator, persuaded me they were worth publishing. To Basil, this book is as much about the journalism of the era as it is about history. He encouraged me to send him some pictures and text so he could do a mock-up of what he thought would work.

Basil could see a book in the now-extinct style from the era of photo-magazine journalism and, using his experience working in the 1960s for *Life* magazine, edited, cropped and laid out my images to bring the best from some of the old, deteriorating transparencies. It was quite unusual for newspaper photographers in the 1950s to take colour, so history from the period can often be visually dull. Basil convinced me that a combination of text detailing such a historic event from a journalist's viewpoint, together with some excellent pictures, would make an interesting book.

It then took another former colleague and mutual friend, Wayne Harman, now managing editor of *The New Zealand Herald*, to set the publishing wheels in motion.

I am also grateful to a former colleague in New York, Todd Pruzan, who joined the conspiracy to persuade me to publish by introducing me to his own literary agents, P J Mark in New York and Caspian Dennis in London.

To back up my own diaries and recollections, I have quoted briefly from the two official accounts of the expedition as well as from the accounts by Sir Edmund Hillary, Rear Admiral George Dufek and George Lowe. These are acknowledged in the text but the full titles of the books are listed here:

Antarctica
by A S Helm and J H Miller
1964, Government Printer, Wellington,
New Zealand

The Crossing of Antarctica
by Sir Vivian Fuchs and Sir Edmund Hillary
1958, Cassell & Company

No Latitude for Error
by Sir Edmund Hillary
1961, Hodder and Stoughton

Operation Deepfreeze
by Rear Admiral George J Dufek
1957, Harcourt, Brace and Company

Because It Is There
by George Lowe
1959, Cassell & Company

The author (right), Sir Edmund and June Hillary catching up on a recent trip to New Zealand.

'You know, Geoff, there's not many of us left,' commented Ed as this photograph was being taken at his home in Auckland, shortly before publication of this book. We had been reminiscing about our small group of companions who had built Scott Base during January 1957.

Sadly the years have taken their toll. Ed has, of course, led an extraordinary life of which the Antarctic jaunt is only a small, although significant part. Of all my memories of him the most enduring is a remark he made to me when returning to New Zealand in 1953, following the Everest climb and after surviving adulatory banquets across Europe.

'I'll be glad to get back to some good, plain New Zealand cooking,' he said disarmingly. I thought at the time it completely defined his down-to-earth character.

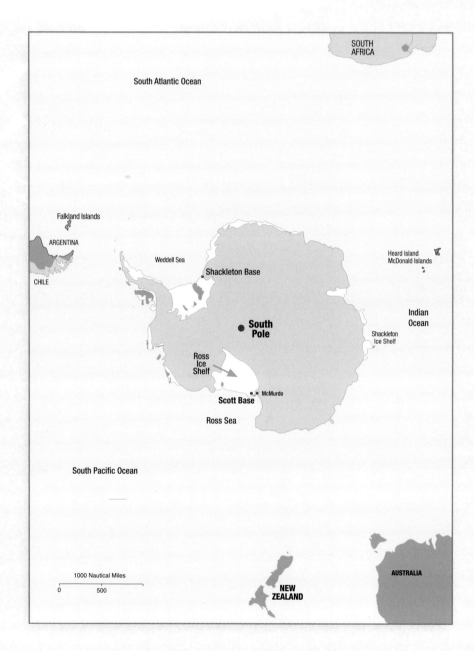

Technical notes

The author took all the images appearing in this book on a 35 mm Kodak Retina II camera, similar to, but much cheaper than, the Leica cameras that were sold in 1956. This format became the standard until the recent arrival of digital cameras.

He shot Kodachrome standard transparency positive film with an ASA rating of only 25, as well as Kodak Verachrome Pan black and white film with an ASA of 64. The Kodachrome of the day was quite remarkable and, other than a few minor adjustments to colour and the removal of dust spots, all these images are as photographed 50 years ago.

Having no formal training in photography, Lee Martin was grateful for tips from Brian Brake, a famed New Zealand photographer working for Magnum and a former staff member of *The New Zealand Herald*. It was Brake who recommended the Retina camera.

Light is so even in the Antarctic that the photographs were usually shot with Kodachrome on f8 at 1/60 for normal light, and one stop up or down for varying conditions. Lee Martin generally used an ultra-violet clear filter when shooting colour, largely to keep the lens clean, and often used an infra-red or orange filter when shooting black and white for better contrast.

Lee Martin also had a Rolliflex, supplied by the trans-Antarctic expedition and, with this, shot dozens of black and white pictures that were issued to the worldwide media, through the New Zealand Press Association and Reuters. Many of the black and white photographs appearing in the official accounts of the expedition were also taken by Lee Martin using this camera, but none carried his by-line.

The Commonwealth Trans-Antarctic Expedition's five-month timetable

1957

5 October:	Dr Vivian Fuchs's party leave their Shackleton Base for reconnaissance of route to South Ice.
14 October:	New Zealand tractor party, led by Sir Edmund Hillary, leaves Scott Base.
20–31 October:	Hillary and team pioneer route up Skelton Glacier to Polar Plateau.
15 November:	Fuchs returns to Shackleton Base.
24 November:	Fuchs leaves Shackleton Base for South Pole six weeks after Hillary's departure from Scott Base.
25 November:	Hillary reaches Depot 480 on the Polar Plateau.
15 December:	Hillary reaches Depot 700, after 'blazing the trail' and establishing depots along the Polar Plateau.
20 December:	Hillary leaves Depot 700 hellbent for the South Pole.
22 December:	Fuchs reaches South Ice, again.
25 December:	Fuchs leaves South Ice for South Pole.

1958

4 January:	Hillary and the Old Firm — Mulgrew, Bates, Ellis and Wright — reach the South Pole.
5 January:	Hillary and three team members are flown back to Scott Base, courtesy of Rear Admiral George Dufek, United States Navy.
18 January:	Dufek flies Hillary and small press party to South Pole to meet Fuchs.
20 January:	Fuchs reaches South Pole, meets Hillary.
24 January:	Fuchs leaves South Pole for Scott Base.
7 February:	Fuchs arrives at Depot 700. Hillary flies back from Scott Base in New Zealand aircraft to guide Fuchs's party.
2 March:	Whole Commonwealth Trans-Antarctic Expedition reaches Scott Base.

Sir Edmund Hillary.

INTRODUCTION

In the week before Christmas, 1957, most of the world's media seemed totally fascinated with what they gleefully dubbed 'the race to the South Pole' between the leaders of the two field parties making up the Commonwealth Trans-Antarctic Expedition: the United Kingdom's Dr Vivian Fuchs (later knighted, after the successful completion of the expedition) and New Zealand's Sir Edmund Hillary, who had recently conquered Mount Everest.

Hillary was, in his own words, 'Hellbent for the Pole', although it had been planned for Fuchs to reach there first.

With four companions aboard three quite basic but reliable Ferguson farm tractors, Hillary had completed his allotted task — laying fuel and food depots toward the Pole to resupply Fuchs's party, which was making the crossing of the continent — but had resolved to press forward.

Back at Scott Base, which the expedition members had built the previous summer to establish a permanent New Zealand presence in Antarctica, I was reporting the growing drama for *The New Zealand Herald* and *The Daily Telegraph* in London, one of a small band of journalists in Antarctica.

Quite determinedly ignoring public advice from officials sitting comfortably in London and Wellington, and some veiled but heavy-handed threats behind the scenes from officials who had no experience of Antarctic conditions, Hillary was pushing on instead of waiting at Depot 700, which was to have been the end of his southern journey — 800 kilometres from the South Pole but more than 1175 kilometres from New Zealand's Scott Base.

The 'Establishment' huffed and puffed and were clearly put out, implying that it was very unsporting of Hillary to get there first!

The initial mission, drawn up in London two years previously, had been for the New Zealand field party to set off in October from Scott Base in McMurdo Sound, due south of New Zealand, to find a route to the Polar Plateau and then lay depots for Fuchs's party, which was crossing via the Pole from its Shackleton Base, south of South America. Hillary's task was necessary because, logistically, Fuchs's party could not carry all the fuel and food needed for their entire journey.

The New Zealanders were to wait at Depot 700 for the British, who — it had been planned — were to be expected within a few days. Then, joined up, both parties were to continue back to Scott Base along the supply depots painstakingly built up by the New Zealanders who had blazed a trail around crevasses, and flown the supplies up to the Polar Plateau by small Beaver and Auster single-engined aircraft.

But that game plan had long since run into difficulties: Fuchs's party had serious problems from the very start while trying to get across the difficult terrain called South Ice near their Shackleton Base. Setting off on the actual traverse seven weeks late, they had also experienced mechanical faults with their Sno-Cat vehicles, which were far more sophisticated than the simple modified Ferguson tractors but untried in Antarctic conditions.

Dr Vivian Fuchs.

By 20 December, when Hillary's support party had completed laying Depot 700, Fuchs's was still more than 1600 kilometres distant, running weeks behind schedule. Hillary then sent Fuchs a radio message saying he had left Depot 700 'with the intention of proving the route another 200 miles [320 km] and then, if the going proves easy, doing the trip to the Pole'.

Hillary's view was that he had little choice but to go on. To stay — as officials back home had suggested — at Depot 700, 2700 metres high on the Polar Plateau and with temperatures often down below minus 30°C would have been to expose the New Zealanders to needless risk.

There was another, potentially serious, factor that did not get much media play but, in retrospect, may have proved crucial to the trans-Antarctic crossing being successfully completed that year. Hillary knew from nerve-wracking experiences that there was a serious crevassed area approaching Depot 700. His tractors had broken through the snow cover on several occasions and, alarmingly, a survey flight by the New Zealand Beaver aircraft beyond Depot 700 indicated there were more crevasses along the planned route Fuchs was to take from the South Pole.

As George Lowe, the New Zealand member of Fuchs's party, recorded later in his book *Because It Is There*: 'Ed radioed Bunny [Fuchs's nickname] offering to clear these crevassed areas so that our path would be marked. Bunny replied: "Okay, go ahead".'

Hillary and his party went ahead marking and preparing the route for Fuchs. Even so, just as they were leaving to explore the crevassed area, Hillary later told me — and I reported — that he had sent a radio message to Fuchs 'offering to scrub the southward jaunt' if Fuchs thought Hillary's party could be of better use elsewhere.

Pack ice in McMurdo Sound, looking north-east towards Ross Island. A volcanic plume from Mount Erebus, 3800 metres, drifts 64 kilometres to Mount Terror, 3260 metres, on the extreme right.

It was more than a week later, Hillary said, when they were 420 kilometres south from Depot 700 and just 390 kilometres from the Pole, that he received a reply from Fuchs asking him to stop and build a Depot 800 'as a precaution'. However, by that time, Hillary's party, with limited fuel and food, was past the point of no return.

By some strange coincidence on 20 December, the day Hillary left Depot 700, he had also received a message from his boss, the chairman of New Zealand's Ross Sea Committee, C M Bowden, asking whether he had received two earlier telegrams dated 5 and 17 December instructing him not to proceed beyond Depot 700. Hillary reacted predictably. 'If an explorer in the field,' he later wrote testily in his memoirs, 'always waited for permission from his committee back home then nothing would get done or it would get done too late. With a grunt I put their message aside.'

Then Hillary — adapting, for more modern conditions, Admiral Lord Nelson's famous tactic at the battle of the Nile of putting his telescope to his blind eye — wrote that he 'seemed to have mislaid the scraps of paper with the messages of the 5th and 17th on them'. He also wrote in his memoirs that he replied to the committee in a somewhat uncompromising tone.

Strengthening Hillary's attitude, Fuchs also reported on the day Hillary left Depot 700 that because of serious crevasse troubles after leaving South Ice (see map on page 19) they had taken 29 days to travel just 562 kilometres. Obviously they had no possibility of reaching the South Pole by even the much-amended date of New Year's Day. As it turned out, Fuchs was still a month away from his eventual arrival at the South Pole on 20 January 1958, and almost seven weeks away from Depot 700. On the other hand, Hillary's party had maintained a tight schedule from the moment they had left Scott Base on 12 October and had kept to

their timetable. The result was that when the New Zealanders arrived at Depot 700 on 15 December 1957, the British were only three weeks into their 11-week journey.

Was it reasonable for Hillary and his men to wait on the Polar Plateau in temperatures that, even in summer, went close to minus 40°C, for an unknown period of time until the British arrived at Depot 700?

The idea that humans should 'camp out' in such conditions was patently absurd. Apart from their using up valuable fuel and food that Fuchs's party needed, at that distance from Scott Base it took the Beaver supply aircraft two gallons of fuel to fly one gallon of fuel in.

Reporting all the action from McMurdo Sound, it seemed absurd to me and I refused to sit on the fence, even though I was writing for audiences of widely diverse opinions in *The New Zealand Herald* and *The Daily Telegraph*. English and New Zealand readers rapidly formed into those who were for Hillary and those who saw his decision as a dastardly attempt to grab the glory from Fuchs and his men.

Hillary's hellbent decision was quite typical of the man who is not, and never has been, a glory-seeker. To others, particularly the jingoistic British tabloid media, his dash was arrogant and uncalled for. The resulting barney stirred up a fine media brawl to enliven the traditional Christmas silly season that, inevitably, became distorted and confused. But it made great copy!

Both official expedition books — *The Crossing of Antarctica* and *Antarctica* — devote many pages to the officials' pros and cons, and large numbers of both British and New Zealand politicians managed to work up quite a sweat. The British media's tone generally was one of condemnation of the uppity colonials, while the New Zealanders naturally took a cautious delight in sticking one up the Poms.

Meanwhile, a whole world away, hellbent it was for Ed Hillary and his men: Peter Mulgrew, then a

navy radio operator and alpinist; Murray Ellis, an engineer and alpinist; Jim Bates, a specialist diesel engineer and also a skilled climbing companion of Hillary; and Derek Wright, a senior cameraman from the New Zealand National Film Unit.

Wright and Mulgrew were close friends of mine and talked to me freely about what went on. Sadly, Peter, who lost his legs from frostbite in the Himalayas two years later after collapsing when almost at the summit of Mount Makalu, was to be killed with all the passengers and crew of an Air New Zealand DC10 that slammed into Mount Erebus during a sightseeing trip to McMurdo Sound on 29 November 1979. And Derek, sadly, also died several years ago.

Sweetening the hellbent decision for the New Zealanders was the offer from Rear Admiral George Dufek, commander of the United States Navy Operation Deepfreeze, to fly Hillary's party back from the Pole to McMurdo Sound in exchange for their trusty Ferguson tractors. All equipment for the Pole station had to be airdropped in and the three tractors would, he said, be most welcome additions to the base equipment.

And this is exactly what happened. The New Zealanders tiredly trundled into the South Pole base on the afternoon of 4 January, and the next day Admiral Dufek arranged for two Neptune aircraft to fly in to pick up Ed and three of his companions — Murray, Jim and Derek — and carry them back to McMurdo Sound. Peter remained at the South Pole station to maintain radio contact between Fuchs and Ed.

Hillary, I felt and wrote, had complete justification to continue on to the Pole. It did not, however, stop the 'Race for the Pole' controversy raging across the international media.

Depot 270, 2440 metres up on the Polar Plateau with a brisk wind blowing. The temperature, I recall, had dropped to about minus 30ºC.

IGY: The scientific reason for all the heroics

The International Geophysical Year (IGY), which was originally planned from 1 July 1957 until 31 December 1958, unofficially began in 1956 and was later extended through 1959. The major purpose of the IGY was to study remote regions, including the Arctic and Antarctic. It was greeted at the time as one of the most significant scientific undertakings in the history of mankind and, in retrospect, it undoubtedly was.

Take just one example, which turned out to be one of the greatest achievements of the 20th century and would have a major impact on all our lives: the launch of the first two primitive satellites.

These were initially intended only to facilitate the study of the upper atmosphere. But their successors — along with the later development of the microchip — soon changed forever the way we communicate, ending our dependence on always unreliable terrestrial radio. They paved the way for a whole new world of instant knowledge and communication.

The IGY was not, however, the first international study of its kind. An International Polar Year had been conducted in 1882–83, when meteorological, magnetic and auroral observation posts were set up in the Arctic. This was followed 50 years later, in 1932–33, by the Second International Polar Year, when ionospheric studies were included. Twenty-five years later, a third — and this time worldwide — International Geophysical Year was decided upon, largely because of scientific advances resulting from the Second World War. Now, a fourth polar year — 2007–08 — is underway.

During the IGY, 64 nations ignored the Cold War to combine and coordinate their scientific studies worldwide for two years. The principal fields of study sound very prosaic these days: solar activity, latitude and longitude, glaciology, oceanography, meteorology, geomagnetism, aurora and airglow, ionospheric physics, seismology and gravity, cosmic rays and, listed last but definitely not least, upper atmosphere rocket and satellite studies.

I say prosaic because it is hard to believe now that, when we went to the Antarctic 50 years ago, we had no reliable means of communication. Voice radio contact between Scott Base and New Zealand was patchy at best, usually interrupted by ionospheric interference — we called it 'sun spots'. Radio 'schedules' needed to be set up so that Scott Base could talk, at designated times, with field parties that, in turn, could rarely communicate with each other.

My newspaper stories, for instance, were sent either by Morse code when reception was difficult, or by radio-teleprinter, which was more reliable but not always infallible, to New Zealand and then relayed on to London. Rolls of black and white photographic film were sent back by infrequent aircraft flights to be developed and printed. No newspaper printed colour photographs.

Many of the IGY studies seem understandable for those times, but why was it necessary to study how to determine latitude and longitude? Had not the invention of the sextant and chronometer solved that? Well, no. These days we have become quite used to various global positioning systems, thanks to satellites, to tell us where we are on our planet, even to the stage of using them instead of a street directory to find our way around an unfamiliar city. My five-year-old granddaughter, for instance, has a small cheap GPS with limited mobile phone facilities which she takes to school. Mother always knows where she is. Fifty years ago we did not even know precisely how far continents were away from each other. Maps of islands frequently contained positioning errors of a mile or more.

Our Commonwealth Trans-Antarctic Expedition was really just a fringe activity, however exciting and glamorous, to the IGY, although both the English and New Zealand elements of the expedition were hosts to scientists who were conducting observations and experiments according to the IGY agenda. In addition, Vivian Fuchs's crossing party took regular seismic, gravimetric and atmospheric readings and there was a scientific group at the United Kingdom's Shackleton Base on the Antarctic Peninsula.

A small group of scientists principally involved in seismic, magnetic and upper atmosphere studies also occupied Scott Base in McMurdo Sound while the New Zealand field parties, particularly the dog teams, did important geological and mapping work as well as similar tasks to those done by Fuchs's crossing party.

In the Antarctic, in preparation for the IGY, the United States had established scientific bases, supported by the United States Navy, at McMurdo, Little America, Byrd, Ellsworth, Wilkes and South Pole stations.

But we were not alone. Other countries participating in the IGY programme around the Antarctic continent were Argentina, Australia, Belgium, Chile, France, Japan, Norway and the Soviet Union. All worked in cooperation, pooling their information.

Virtually nothing was known about satellites that, according to the scientists, would be tricky to place in orbit and were quite likely to fly off into space. No rocket had yet been built that was powerful enough to put even a very small payload into orbit.

The United States, which was assumed to lead

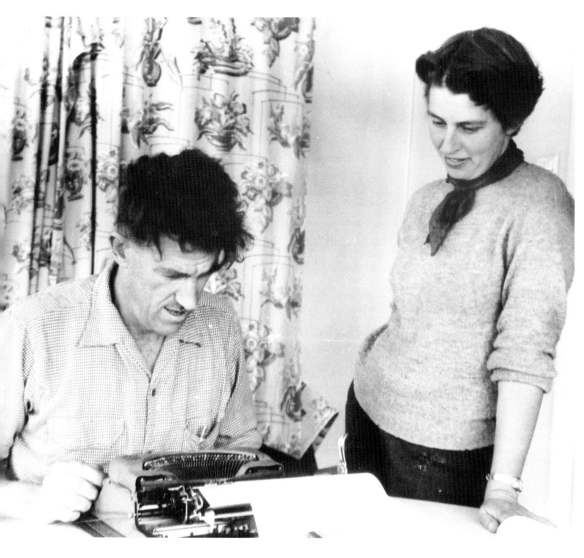

I took this shot of Ed Hillary, with his wife Louise, working on his book of the expedition after we returned to Auckland in 1958. Ed told me his writing routine was to 'peck out' a first draft, revise it and then type a final copy.

The International Geophysical Year, which opened up the continent and proved that humans could live there safely, led to an orderly colonisation and exploration by a number of nations.

Inevitably, it has also led, in recent years, to a rush of adventure-seekers, fortified by the certainty that Antarctica is no longer an unknown continent and quite easy to access — and anxious to demonstrate their ability to reach the South Pole by one bizarre method or another.

Don't misunderstand me: I make a distinction here between the jingoistic heroic era and the genuine heroes who often did not seek or receive public acclaim, even if they occasionally got it.

And I remember quite vividly a conversation Ed Hillary's first wife Louise told me she had with Mrs Cherry-Garrard, widow of Apsley Cherry-Garrard, a member of Scott's last expedition. He is best remembered for his book *The Worst Journey in the World*, a gripping account of a journey — made during the depths of winter from Hut Point in McMurdo Sound to the Cape Crozier penguin rookery on the far side of Ross Island — that is a classic of Polar travel.

'At least you will know, by newspaper accounts and occasional radio telephone conversations, what is happening,' Mrs Cherry-Garrard said to Lady Hillary. 'When we waved goodbye to our men as the ship left the wharf we knew we would hear nothing more until — or perhaps, if — they returned in two or three years' time.'

Sadly, Louise and the Hillarys' younger daughter Belinda, who was born about the same time as my daughter Bridget, died in an aircraft accident in the Himalayas on 31 March 1975, while visiting one of Hillary's projects building schoolhouses for the Sherpa people.

in satellite research, planned to put as many as a dozen spheres — 50 centimetres in diameter and weighing about 10 kilograms — into orbit in 1957, calling their project 'Earth Satellite No. 1' but they were experiencing delays. These satellites were hoped to supplement a much larger programme to launch 600 rockets that, it was said, would provide crucial information about the upper atmosphere, even though their flights would be of limited duration.

It came as a stunning shock, therefore, when the Soviet Union quite unexpectedly blasted the first satellite, which they called Sputnik, into orbit on 4 October 1957. Across the world millions gazed nightly up at the skies to catch a glimpse of Sputnik's tiny glow as it raced past, and listened to the strangely haunting 'beep, beep, beep' of its radio signal. Clearly it was felt something very significant had happened.

It was four months later before the United States launched its first primitive satellite on 31 January 1958, and by then the space race was most definitely on, culminating 11 years later on 20 July 1969 when man first landed on the moon. For those interested in trivial information, that was Sir Edmund Hillary's 50th birthday.

At the time Sputnik went up I was preparing to make the first flight from Christchurch to the Antarctic for the 1957–58 summer with Rear Admiral George Dufek, commander of the United States Operation Deepfreeze, and the Americans' reaction to the Russian triumph was painful to watch.

Returning to McMurdo, with George Dufek, 12 October 1957

Flying south on the 13-hour trip from Christchurch to McMurdo with Rear Admiral George Dufek in his 'personal' Navy Douglas DC4 Skymaster aircraft on 12 October 1957 — we were lunching, I recall, on rare chateaubriand steak about 2400 metres above the pack ice — I noticed the pilot, Lieutenant Commander Harold Hansen, come into the cabin and whisper in George's ear. Was something wrong?

Well yes, if you were an American concerned about the coming 'space race'. The Russian Sputnik — the first man-made object in space — had gone up a week earlier and Hansen had picked up its eerie radio signal as it was passing overhead. At the Admiral's request, the sound was broadcast throughout the cabin until it faded away, and conversation stopped as we contemplated what it might mean.

Even then, nearly 12 years before an American finally landed on the moon, we were all very conscious that space exploration was going to be, to borrow a phrase not yet coined by Trekkies, the next challenging frontier. The IGY was laying the groundwork.

That summer, scientific teams from Cambridge University and what was to become the United States space agency spent several weeks in McMurdo Sound, studying both the conditions there and the way individuals — using us all as guinea pigs when they got the chance — reacted to harsh environments.

On one occasion, the Cambridge team wired several of us up to instruments, subjected us to all sorts of uncomfortable conditions and, in my case at least, came to the conclusion that my metabolic rate resembled that of an emperor penguin. I don't know how valuable this was, although I gather that while it might mean I withstood cold well it also might explain why I've had a continual battle with my weight as I've got older.

One conclusion they did come to was that the surface of the dry valleys in the mountain ranges

Admiral Dufek's 'personal' DC4 aircraft in which we flew to McMurdo Sound on 12 October 1957.

on the western side of McMurdo could resemble the surface of the moon. This eventually proved to be correct and was apparently quite valuable in the design of vehicles for the initial space landings.

Not everyone was convinced that space travel was possible, however.

My editor at *The New Zealand Herald,* the formidable OS Budge Hintz, was one who thought it all nonsense. A few days before I flew south with Dufek he joined me and a group of colleagues in the staff cafeteria and asked genially what the scientists were planning to do down there.

When I started to explain about the scientists' interest in space travel, Budge grew purple in the face, snapped 'Don't be so bloody silly', picked up his cup of tea and stalked away while the rest of us looked at each other in amazement.

More than a decade later, when I was acting as news editor at the *Herald* one night, Budge dropped in after dinner as he usually did to ask what news was breaking. By this time he had accepted space travel but did not understand the mechanics of it. When I told him that the American astronauts were about to begin the first space walk his reaction was again baffling. 'But they'll all fall down,' he said. Budge was an intelligent man who wrote beautifully but, like quite a few others at the time, just could not comprehend the rapid changes that were taking place in our world.

Most of my expedition colleagues and I firmly believed that space travel was just around the corner and, perhaps, that colonisation of the moon would happen in my lifetime. I well

remember looking up at the full moon one clear night after returning home and thinking that I might eventually get up there myself, working on my Antarctic experiences. Alas, all those hopes still remain unrealised.

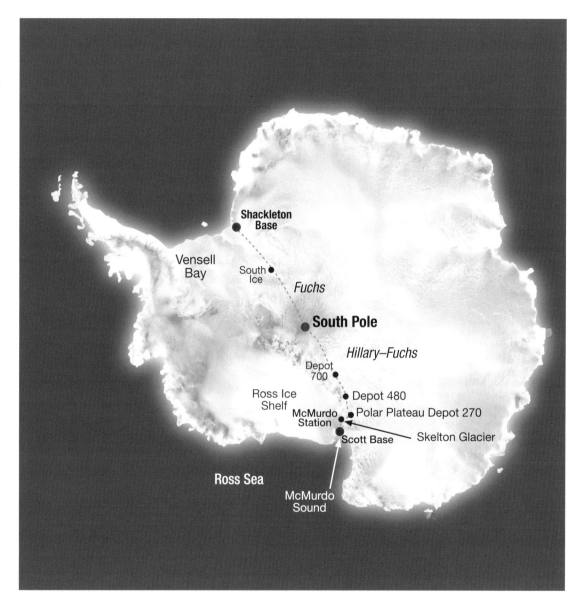

A satellite's view of the Antarctic, showing the route of the Commonwealth Trans-Antarctic Expedition, the bases and depots.

FUCHS, HILLARY AND DUFEK

Three men of complex but very different characters met at the South Pole on 20 January 1958 — Dr Vivian Fuchs and Rear Admiral George Dufek, United States Navy, both veterans of many years of Antarctic and Arctic exploration, and Sir Edmund Hillary whose snow and ice experiences had predominantly been in high mountains. In another more romantic era all might have been called men of destiny.

Vivian Fuchs, 49, a powerfully built, jaunty six-footer, swung down from the leading Sno-Cat as Ed Hillary, 38, broke from our group and walked towards him, calling out 'Hullo, Bunny'. Although about 10 centimetres taller, Hillary looked tired and rather gaunt, still recovering from carbon monoxide poisoning caused by a faulty tractor exhaust during his dash to the Pole.

Fuchs almost ran to the New Zealander. 'Hullo, Ed,' he replied. 'Damned glad to see you.' And the pair shook hands warmly.

Above: *Ed Hillary on 5 January, a few minutes after arriving back in McMurdo Sound. He and his party had reached the South Pole the previous day. Dufek had offered to fly Hillary and his companions back from the Pole in return for leaving their three Ferguson tractors there.*

Left: *Vivian Fuchs, left, and George Dufek standing alongside Fuchs's Sno-Cat a few minutes after the British party arrived at the South Pole on 20 January 1958.*

Watching, along with me and a small group of assorted newsmen and United States naval personnel, was George Dufek, 55, also powerfully built, though stocky and several inches shorter than either Fuchs or Hillary. Dufek had made this meeting possible and yet was the unheralded and largely unacknowledged guardian angel to the Commonwealth Trans-Antarctic Expedition.

No one, certainly at that moment, seemed to remember that it was Dufek who had, only two years earlier, been the first man to stand on the South Pole since Scott and his four companions 44 years before, or that he and the six United States airmen with him had achieved this feat by pioneering an extremely hazardous landing and equally perilous take-off in a small but wondrously versatile Douglas DC3 passenger aircraft called *Que Sera Sera*, adapted by the navy with skis and JATO (jet-assisted take-off) bottles of rocket fuel.

This perhaps was the defining moment when the heroic era of exploration ended and the great adventure of colonisation of the Antarctic by scientists became a reality.

Fuchs and Hillary's greeting was also a clue to the complex, often puzzling, character of Fuchs who was a genuinely dedicated explorer in the tradition of Scott. Like Scott, the Royal Navy captain, he was a rather remote leader who stuck stubbornly to what he believed was right and, like Scott, he seldom sought advice.

Scott blundered badly, said polar scientist

A favourite topic of debate, among old, or new, Antarctic explorers, is comparing the widely differing characters of Scott and Shackleton, their leadership abilities, or lack of abilities and — more often than not — just how successful they really were.

A couple of months before Hillary and Fuchs set off, Sir Raymond Priestley, a scientist with Scott in the Antarctic, got a lot of people in England hot under the collar by asserting Scott and his men lost their race to the Pole and their lives, because their methods 'were less than the best'. Priestley made his surprise criticism while addressing the British Association for the Advancement of Science, of which he was then president:

We did most of the approach work [to the Pole] *and were beaten to the post because we did not fully understand the value of dogs as transport animals, nor how to get the best out of those we used.*

Other factors contribute to the tragedy but the stark fact is that, with sledging rations completely devoid of vitamin C, the margin of safety of any man-hauling party to the South Pole from any base on the rim of the continent was too small.

Scott committed errors of organisation for which he more than atoned by the manner of his death.

He should not have changed his party from two units of four men to one of three and one of five. By doing so he endangered the party going back who had, without measuring or weighing apparatus, to take exactly three quarters of the food [from dozens of weekly bags of food supplies left at the return depots].

He handicapped his own party psychologically by crowding them into a tent meant for four men and disorganised a very carefully thought out routine. He made, in my opinion, a bad mistake in taking with him three officers and one long-service seaman, who was in a thought-tight compartment by himself and was naturally the first to break.

Acknowledging that the weather during the summer of 1911–12 was unusual and unkind — it has since been recognised as one of the worst summers recorded — Priestley said 'Nevertheless, scurvy was, I believe, the decisive factor. Under man-hauling conditions, four months is about as long as men hauling sledges can live on rations completely devoid of vitamin C.'

Obviously not helping, either, was their decision to carry back about 16 kilograms of rock specimens collected on their way down the Beardmore Glacier. But it is fair to let Peter Scott, Robert Scott's son, have the last word:

In pointing out, a long time after the event, things that might have been done differently, my friend Sir Raymond Priestley has expressed opinions which he is fully entitled and fully qualified to give. I have no doubt my father would have agreed with him, had he been able to look back on events.

But I hardly think that, by pointing out some of the factors which may have led to the tragic end of the Polar party, Sir Raymond remotely intended to — or has, in fact, said anything to — destroy the Scott legend.

The debate will continue.

It apparently did not occur to Fuchs that his companions or anyone else would appreciate a closer day-to-day knowledge of the task being done. For example, during the height of the controversy between himself and Hillary, the only inkling his companions had that something was brewing was through an occasional news broadcast picked up from the BBC, highlighting once again the great communications handicap we battled 50 years ago, before satellites.

George Lowe, who had been with Hillary on Everest, told me later that they were completely in the dark about any exchanges of messages between Fuchs and Hillary and finally they had to tell Fuchs bluntly that they would appreciate being put in the picture. To Fuchs's credit, he responded readily: it presumably had not entered his mind that they should be told. In George's autobiography *Because It Is There*, he says revealingly:

The word went around in one of our more impudent and disrespectful whispers, 'Matron wants to see you all before school begins' when Fuchs called the meeting. After reading the messages Bunny said there was no question of our not continuing the journey, there was no discussion of either the messages or his decision — and we drove on.

Later, Lowe describes Fuchs as 'enigmatic, [a man] whose inner motives baffled us'. Yet Fuchs was, in his public persona at least, a dedicated scientist 'making a polar traverse' to gain further knowledge of the continent. If, in his heart of hearts, he also realised it was an historic expedition of some significance, he did not mention it to any of us.

While he definitely had his remote side, he could be extremely human. He was at his genial best after arriving at the Pole and I wrote at the time that the girls in his English office thought he was wonderful and would do almost anything for him. Equally, while he brooked no breaking of his rules, he was quite prepared to break the rules of others.

In England, for instance, he took a favourite husky everywhere, regardless.

When we met, Fuchs was puzzled that there had been pandemonium in the world's media. This hullabaloo was because Hillary's team — the support group — had reached the Pole before his trans-Antarctic party, and also because Hillary had then recommended (because summer was ending and there were many miles of crevassed areas still to be crossed) that Fuchs postpone the final leg to Scott Base until the following summer.

Fuchs knew clearly that his was the absolute and final responsibility for getting the trans-Antarctic party to safety. He made this plain when he told me shortly after arriving at the South Pole, 'Ed was doing his duty when he gave me his evaluation of our chances. He made a suggestion to stop at the South Pole and I did not accept it. There was no argument.'

In stark contrast there was Hillary, an adventurer, man of Everest and a national hero in the mould of Shackleton — a dashing, brilliant leader with a flair

Waiting at the South Pole on 20 January 1958 for the British party to arrive: Lieutenant Vernon Houk, the military leader (left), Sir Edmund (centre) and Major Palle (Moggie) Morgensen, the scientific chief (right). All the American bases in Antarctica had dual leadership.

for doing the popular thing — who cheerfully called his long, hazardous trek with farm tractors to the Pole a 'jaunt'.

There was no argument, however, about who was running the New Zealand end. Fuchs emphasised in an interview with me that he was perfectly happy for Hillary to go on to the Pole from Depot 700, contrary to everything we media hacks had written about the 'feud'.

I still find it fascinating to recall the small details of that meeting at the South Pole on a cloudless, windless and brilliantly sunny day with the temperature hovering around a comfortable minus 20°C.

George Dufek linked arms and walked with the two men into the United States Navy's Amundsen Scott Station for a hearty breakfast. They were chatting like old friends as they seriously discussed the task Fuchs still faced if he was to reach Scott Base, 2000 kilometres away, before the approaching winter locked them in. After all, Fuchs's party had covered only slightly more than 1440 kilometres to date, and time was running out.

Vivian Fuchs, who would have his 50th birthday on the Polar Plateau the following month, looked like an explorer. I described him at the time as a big man but his deep blue eyes, peering out under shaggy eyebrows that were almost too good to be true, dominated. He was the son of a Thuringian German who migrated to England (when Fuchs was seven) and became a prosperous Kent farmer.

Fuchs attended St John's College, Cambridge, a famous breeding ground for explorers, and when he was 21 went on his first expedition to East Greenland as a geologist. Later he also travelled on three expeditions to East Africa before completing his thesis on the geology of the Rift Valley for a doctorate. In the late 1930s he married, had a son and a daughter, and as a young geologist was set to become involved in oil exploration, but the war intervened. He served in Africa and Europe, rising to

the rank of major, and was mentioned in dispatches.

His die was cast when the United Kingdom became involved in a bitter conflict with Argentina and Chile over claims to the Graham Land Peninsula (shots were fired, preceding the much more lethal conflict 20 years later) and set up the Falkland Island Dependencies Survey in 1947 (they called it FIDS). Dr Fuchs was appointed its leader.

Just to confuse the issue, Graham Land, named by the British naval captain Edward Bransfield in January 1820, after a Lord of the Admiralty at that time, is called Palmer Peninsula by the Americans after Nathaniel Palmer who, they claim, actually discovered the Antarctic continent. However, Palmer sighted the coast 10 months after Bransfield, in November 1820.

In 1948, marooned in Graham Land for the bitter Antarctic winter when the relief ship *John Biscoe* could not penetrate the sea ice, Fuchs conceived the idea of finally achieving Shackleton's plan for crossing the Antarctic continent which — how times change — was called the Imperial Trans-Antarctic Expedition. By the oddest of coincidences the *John Biscoe* was transformed into *Endeavour*, the little ship that transported the New Zealand contingent of the Commonwealth Trans-Antarctic Expedition to McMurdo Sound.

In the following years Fuchs wintered three times in Antarctica on the Falklands side, and sledged thousands of kilometres across Graham Land, gaining so much experience that, by the time he began pushing publicly in 1950 to create a trans-Antarctic expedition, he probably knew more about living and working on the continent than any other person alive.

Ed Hillary, by contrast, became a renowned mountaineer almost by accident. His father, a newspaper man, had been invalided home during the First World War and eventually took up beekeeping to live a more healthy outdoor life, helped by Ed and

his brother, Rex. Ed attended Auckland Grammar and went on skiing trips. Shortly after he started university the Second World War intervened and Ed joined up, serving as a navigator in Royal New Zealand Air Force Catalina flying boats in the Pacific; coincidentally, one of my cousins was his pilot.

Ed was severely burned in a boating accident while still on active duty, shortly after the war ended, and during his recuperation back in New Zealand found there was little for a beekeeper to do during the winter. New Zealand's Southern Alps were beckoning.

The mountaineering bug bit hard and soon he was climbing in the European Alps. In 1951 he was invited to join Shipton's Everest expedition. The rest is mountaineering history and formed Hillary's life-long love of the Himalayas and the Sherpa people. At the time of the expedition he was married with a son and daughter. A second girl came along later.

And what sort of man was George Dufek? He had an extraordinary career as an active ship's submariner, a naval aviator and veteran of two previous Antarctic expeditions. He also had a distinguished wartime career and a passion for trout fishing. His wife and two young sons lived more or less permanently in Christchurch for the duration of his command of Operation Deepfreeze.

For a long time Dufek was under the shadow of Rear Admiral Richard Byrd, who had stamped his personality and authority over recent Antarctic exploration — from the Americans' perspective at least. George had been with Byrd on his 1939–41 expedition as navigator of the *Bear* and undertook many hours of exploratory flying over the Antarctic continent between Little America and the Palmer Peninsula. Only after Byrd's death in 1957 was Dufek officially acknowledged as commander of all United States Antarctic programmes.

During the war he had coordinated the airborne units involved in the invasion of Sicily and Italy, then helped plan the amphibious invasion of southern France. Soon after the war ended he was back in the Antarctic commanding a seaplane squadron attached to Operation Highjump in 1946–47, during which a taskforce led by Admiral Byrd again explored the continent. George made the first flights over the Thurston Peninsula and the Bellingshausen Sea — the region where Fuchs also explored and later built his Shackleton Base.

Dufek had a swag of military and civilian decorations, among them the Distinguished Service Medal, the Legion of Merit with two gold stars, the Croix de Guerre and Legion of Honor, and even the Andre Medal from the Swedish government. There is a stretch of coastline named after him along New Zealand's Ross Sea Dependency.

But when he retired in 1960 the honour he cherished most was his appointment as director of the Mariners' Museum in Newport News, Virginia, which is dedicated to the preservation and advancement of all the arts and sciences related to the sea. The best thing about the post, George told me in a Christmas card that year, was the great trout-fishing streams nearby!

I cherish something Dufek once said, referring to the many achievements, that he and others had realised, including so many firsts, and I believe it typifies the man: 'It is not the actual doing of it that is difficult. The great accomplishment is the imagination, planning and hard work of the many people needed to prepare for it.'

George Dufek, Ed Hillary and Bunny Fuchs were three remarkable men indeed. To me, at our meeting at the South Pole 10 years after the great trans-Antarctic dream began, there was one last clue to the character of the man called Vivian Ernest Fuchs: on his passport he described himself as 'explorer'. By contrast, Ed Hillary's passport described him as 'beekeeper'— I know because I looked.

The modest entrance to the Amundsen–Scott South Pole Station, with the Americans' scientific observation dome rising above the snow drifts.

The heroic era was a Victorian concept

Brave men — no women, naturally — went off to the ends of the earth (usually deepest Africa or exotic Asia but occasionally, if the Congo or Outer Mongolia was getting a trifle crowded, to the Arctic or Antarctic).

It was a concept that fitted a time when nations were seeking to expand their world domination: what better than to revive the legendary heroic ages of ancient Greece and Rome when heroes sought glory, defined in my dictionary as a 'response to the challenges of destiny and the gods'. To qualify, a Victorian hero was intrepid, determined and, more often than not, a tad foolhardy.

Looking back, it is refreshingly clear that the Commonwealth Trans-Antarctic Expedition emphatically ruled a line under the heroic-era concept of Antarctic exploration that developed and grew with the exploits of Scott, Shackleton, Amundsen, Byrd, and, before them Bellingshausen, Balleny, Ross, Borchgrevink and others, including many whalers still unsung, who were merely seeking wealth.

But there were many die-hards both in the United Kingdom and New Zealand who found it difficult to let go. After all, there was the great British tradition of exploration to defend.

Vivian Fuchs found this out when he began his one-man campaign to launch what was to become the 1956–58 Commonwealth Trans-Antarctic Expedition. He must have been staggered by the scorn and downright hostility from other scientists and so-called polar experts, who, it would have been reasonable for him to expect, should have been supportive.

But, as someone else wrote at the time, explorers and scientists are curiously human and are just as susceptible to meanness, jealousy and short-sightedness as everyone else.

The Scott Polar Research Institute was not even slightly interested in supporting Fuchs's plan. And, even more surprisingly, the trans-Antarctic expedition did not go under the auspices of the Royal Geographical Society although the society later scrambled on to the bandwagon.

Fuchs's dream might not have got off the ground at all if it had not been for the enthusiastic support of a prominent British explorer, Sir James Wordie, who had been chief scientist with Shackleton's expedition.

But his first real support came in 1954 when Sir Winston Churchill, then Prime Minister, found time to listen and arranged to have Fuchs outline his plan at that year's Conference of Commonwealth Prime Ministers, who immediately saw the possibilities and prestige that could be achieved.

Churchill pledged £100,000 sterling. New Zealand's Prime Minister, Sir Walter Nash, was also enthusiastic, initially pledging £50,000 sterling, which eventually grew to a staggering contribution of about £250,000 in cash and kind from the New Zealand public. Australia promised £18,000 and South Africa £12,000.

Fuchs was at last off and running.

Relaxing in the warmth of the mess hut at Scott Base. Bob Holmes Miller (centre) was Ed Hillary's quiet but forceful and extremely respected deputy who, with George Marsh, accomplished one of the greatest ever polar journeys with dog teams. On the left is Guy Warren, a surveyor who also worked with a dog team in the mountains.

Our tough little Auster aircraft experienced early what it was likely to meet in the Antarctic while we were training high up on the Tasman Glacier in the Southern Alps in New Zealand. It was buried during a sudden snowstorm and took a day to dig out.

CHAPTER
2

A CALL FROM SIR EDMUND

Around the middle of 1956 I received a phone call from Ed Hillary. This wasn't unusual because we had been in regular, sometimes almost daily, contact since he had returned to Auckland after climbing Mount Everest two-and-a-half years earlier. But what he said was unusual, at least to me: 'Geoff, we've been talking about this jaunt to the Antarctic. Applications to join the expedition close pretty soon but I haven't seen one from you, yet.'

I was stunned. I'd never thought of myself as a potential explorer — intrepid or otherwise — although I was a keen skier and had some mountaineering experience. After we hung up, I gradually became elated as I thought about what a great adventure it would be. I remember that one of the first things I did was go out and buy Scott's diaries and one or two other volumes available about the Antarctic in second-hand bookstores.

It wasn't as hard as I had figured to convince my editor to give me leave to apply — he clearly thought it was an honour for the newspaper, but it was only after my application was accepted that I began to realise some of the complications of being both a journalist and an expedition member.

My association with Hillary had begun three years earlier when my news editor at the time, a crusty but superb journalist called Claude Tendall, strode into the reporters' room and called out: 'Anyone know anything about this chap Hillary? He looks like he might be about to climb Everest.' When there was dead silence I admitted that I knew a bit about him. 'Good,' said Claude, 'write me a backgrounder just in case he gets to the top.' So I made a few phone calls, went out to see Ed's parents, who lived near where I did, and wrote a potted biography that was later used in the *Herald* and, in more abbreviated form, by *The Daily Telegraph*.

Now, with the Antarctic venture looming, Ed was putting together a very tight party, chosen from hundreds of applicants by exhaustive sub-committees but with his clear involvement. Ed wanted every member having several skills that would be useful, as well as their regular discipline. Some surprising extra talents, or hobbies, were eventually unearthed, especially during the long, sunless winter months that included gourmet cooking, debating, acting, painting, model-making and even knitting.

In all, 18 field party members and scientists, including Ed, were chosen to winter-over for the full term. Fourteen more, including me, went down for the 1956–57 summer season, charged with helping build Scott Base and becoming the support team.

Ed Hillary and the author having a yarn during a quiet moment at Scott Base. I had seized the opportunity to get some quotes for publication about how the stocking of the supply depots on the Skelton Glacier was proceeding.

My main duty, naturally, was to report our activities, which meant I needed freedom to range around, but Ed cheerfully told me that as I also wrote a weekly motoring page for the *Herald* he expected me to be a competent tractor driver! And that's what I became, and thoroughly enjoyed, after demonstrating my ability during our training in the Southern Alps. I also tried my hand once or twice at cooking Sunday dinner when Buck Bucknell, our cook, had a day off.

As I was the only reporter with the trans-Antarctic expedition, the arrangement, which needed negotiation with the *Herald*, was that I wrote for the New Zealand Press Association. It would syndicate my stories throughout New Zealand and overseas through its Reuters-associated network.

This worked very well as far as the expedition went, but the *Herald* became unhappy at my not being able to write exclusively for them and so, as I recount elsewhere, I became accredited to the United States Navy's Operation Deepfreeze the following summer (1957–58) when the real drama of the trans-Antarctic crossing began to mount.

From August 1956 onward, my preparation for the coming adventure included several weeks training with most of the team getting really fit in New Zealand's Southern Alps, based at the Malte Brun Hut high above the Tasman Glacier, under Mount Cook.

In addition to that exercise, some specialist expedition members gained extra training elsewhere. For instance, our doctor George Marsh, an Englishman, took a dentistry course as a precaution, even though it had been necessary for all of us to pass a tough medical and dental examination. And, Buck swotted up on cooking for masses: first the basic skills at an army cookery school and then a touch of gourmet cooking in a posh Wellington hotel.

Working on a flat area of shoreline near Wellington's Rongotai Airport, the base construction crew got more experience than they had expected when they tested their skills in assembling one of the prefabricated huts we took down to create Scott Base. It was winter and as they slogged to get the hut up they were sometimes lashed by gales and rain. Chastened, they warned us direly about what we were likely to encounter. But their fears were unfounded: weather during the actual construction in McMurdo Sound was, we all thanked the gods who look after Antarctic travellers, quite different — calm and mostly sunny throughout.

On the Tasman Glacier we gained experience with the huskies and learned a lot more about the dangers of crevasses. Ed and eight key members of the proposed field parties had already been working the huskies, getting them accustomed to pulling sledges in cold weather — down to minus 30°C of frost on the glacier at night.

Even getting to Malte Brun Hut, perched dramatically by some humorist, or maybe sadist, on a rocky ledge 150 metres above the glacier, was a sobering initial test of our abilities for many of us, and I'm sure Ed planned it that way. His official line, though, was that the glacier area stretching around the hut was very nearly flat, about three kilometres wide and 13 kilometres long — making it ideal to train the huskies and get used to our aircraft.

To get to the hut, we first walked on skis about eight kilometres up the glacier through the snow with backpacks, a testing exercise for men who had come straight from desks in city offices. Confronting the climb to the hut, it brought home just how unfit I really was. Clambering up the near vertical slope from the glacier to the hut, trying to keep in the footsteps of the man in front, had those of us who were not seasoned mountaineers wondering — during pauses to gasp for breath in the rarefied alpine air — what life was going to be like in the Antarctic. Happily we were to discover that, by comparison, Scott Base resembled a pleasant, if basic, ski village.

Then to work, which included learning how to use all our equipment. One jaunt — to borrow Ed's phrase — which I found to be rather pleasant, was to slog three or four kilometres further up the glacier to its saddle and camp out for the night, carrying survival gear. We had to choose a camping site, erect a tent and cook a meal on a primus stove using basic rations before rolling into a sleeping bag for the night.

Testing radio communications between our aircraft and ground parties got particular emphasis. Radio gear to be used on the Polar Plateau was installed at Malte Brun and fine-tuned to be able to communicate with larger transmitters in Wellington, a distance of about 650 kilometres which was thought to be the equivalent direct-line distance from Scott Base to the Plateau. The base transmitters to be installed also needed to be able to send Morse, radio pictures and radio-telephone conversations back to New Zealand.

We took the opportunity to test and make quite a few adjustments to the clothing that had been issued for the trip. One fault, it soon became obvious to many of us, was that the clothing manufacturers had apparently assumed we were all the same size as Ed Hillary, who was 1.9 metres tall and quite large. Most of the clothing, especially shirts, sweaters, anoraks and so on, was quickly replaced and our wives, mothers or girlfriends also had some serious nipping and tucking to do when we returned home. But our boots and other footwear were first class and became the envy of American personnel we met up with at McMurdo.

We also got some practical experience we hadn't expected. While landing our Auster, which in hindsight seemed accident prone, on the glacier late in the afternoon one of our pilots struck a rough patch and the aircraft flipped over. We turned it back on to its skis, but a storm was brewing so we secured and left the aircraft until the next day, only to find it almost covered in newly fallen snow. Carefully digging it out took almost a day.

Planning for the trans-Antarctic expedition had been going on, behind the scenes, since mid-1955, when the British and New Zealand committees formed to steer the expedition got down to serious work and fund-raising began.

During the southern summer of 1955–56, one year before we sailed south on *Endeavour*, a number of advance sorties were made to the Antarctic by both British and New Zealand expedition members to prepare for the main journey.

Ed Hillary, Bob Miller and Squadron Leader John Claydon, our chief pilot, joined Vivian Fuchs and nine other Britons (most of whom were to winter-over) on *Theron*, a ship supplying British Falklands Dependency bases in the Weddell Sea. They had a fairly tough time of it, breaking through a difficult barrier of pack ice before getting clear to establish the site for Shackleton Base, the British jumping-off point for the polar journey. Ed's surprise phone call to me was made just after he returned from this trip.

Once on land, Ed and Bob had the opportunity to test Ferguson tractors equipped with half tracks in Antarctic conditions for the first time and found them wanting in some aspects, especially in soft snow. At this stage, Ed was still working on the composition of the field teams to lay the depots and do survey work, and was placing great importance on huskies.

This changed upon their return to Europe when they visited a Norwegian company that had been modifying Ferguson tractors. After testing various possibilities they decided to fit out the Fergusons with full tracks, and that is what we finally took south. In this configuration the front wheels were centrally locked and tracks were fitted joining the front and rear wheels. Steering was achieved by braking either side using hand levers, rather than a steering wheel. In practice, our four sturdy, simply built Fergusons worked surprisingly well and, to the joy of our mechanics, needed very little serious maintenance.

Meanwhile, Bernie Gunn, a geologist and skilled mountaineer, Dr Trevor Hatherton, New Zealand's IGY leader and a geophysicist, and Lieutenant Commander Bill Smith, RNZN, were spending the summer in and around McMurdo Sound as the guests of the Americans there, seeking out and inspecting possible sites for Scott Base, learning at first hand about the working conditions in the area and coordinating New Zealand's IGY plans with those of the United States.

And, intent on gathering as much knowledge about the Antarctic as possible, Harry Ayres was visiting Mawson, an Australian Antarctic base on the coast a few thousand kilometres west of McMurdo.

Harry, a senior guide in the Southern Alps, was famous throughout the international world of mountaineering for his snow and ice techniques and was an expert with huskies. He and Hillary had met nine years before when Ed was just learning mountaineering crafts and Harry taught him all he knew. They remained close friends. 'He took me under his wing and for three marvellous seasons we climbed the big peaks together,' Ed wrote in his book *High Adventure*.

The mothers of New Zealand, and many of their daughters, were busy too. Warm woollen mittens and socks were knitted in profusion. For instance, Mrs O'Reilly and a bevy of friends spun wool at home from fleece that had won a championship award at Auckland's Easter Show (then a national forum for farming produce), including one pair of black mittens, especially for Ed, from the O'Reillys' pet sheep. Ordinary woollen products, Mrs O'Reilly maintained, would not be tough enough for the Antarctic!

And in scores of cities, towns and hamlets, community groups organised galas and other special events to sell all sorts of products — lamingtons, sponge cakes and pavlova being most popular — to raise money for the Antarctic appeal. In a staggering way, the whole country swung behind the project.

Strange things were also beginning to occur to the wheels of government, heralded by a solemn announcement from the New Zealand Governor-General: as we were planning to build a base and explore the Ross Dependency, a territory legally administered by New Zealand, it was thought necessary to prepare for possible contingencies, whatever they might be. Ed Hillary was gazetted a stipendiary magistrate and postmaster, Trevor Hatherton became a justice of the peace and a coroner and Captain Kirkwood from *Endeavour* was appointed general deputy to the administrator of the dependency as well as a stipendiary magistrate and, of all things, 'nautical advisor to the Marine Department'.

This was beginning to look serious!

We celebrated Christmas 1956 on 29 December when Endeavour *parked against a large ice floe. After a sumptuous luncheon we stretched our legs on the ice. The Auster is on the back of the ship without its wings following an accident at Lyttelton Harbour. Edmund Hillary is in the foreground on the left.*

CHAPTER 3

THE GOOD SHIP *ENDEAVOUR*

The day before our expedition sailed from Wellington Harbour on 15 December 1956, Pamela (my first wife) and I went down to the wharves to load my gear and to inspect, for the first time, *Endeavour*, the wooden-hulled vessel that was to take us to McMurdo Sound.

We found the wharf but it seemed unoccupied, with no ship in sight, so we asked a passing stevedore for directions. 'There she is,' he said, pointing to where two bare masts rose above the far end of the wharf decking.

With some surprise and, I confess, mounting trepidation, we walked to the edge and there below us, with the tide out, she lay — the small, 900-tonne ship that was to carry us some 1600 kilometres through the notoriously fierce Southern Ocean and pack ice to Antarctica. I'm unsure how I looked but I know Pamela was not very impressed. *Endeavour* looked to be not much bigger than a harbour tug. Indeed, that had been her first role.

I tried to reassure Pamela. *Endeavour*, I explained, was a veteran of Antarctic waters. Having been bought from the Royal Navy in 1947 by the Falkland Islands government and renamed the *John Biscoe*, she had been used to service the bases that the United Kingdom maintained on the Falklands' Antarctic coast.

Endeavour had been built in 1944 in the United States, named HMS *Pretext* and used in wartime in the United Kingdom as a harbour defence net layer. She had virtually no keel — which, as we soon found out, made her roll spectacularly, even in moderately calm weather, but which was supposed to ensure that if she were caught in pack ice she would avoid being crushed by popping up out of the sea. To make her sturdier, her hull had been sheathed in green-heart timber.

I don't think I reassured Pamela very much, but there was a stout gangplank leading to the deck at a sharp angle and we clambered down. A naval rating came up, saluted smartly and led us off to meet the ship's executive officer, Lieutenant Commander Bill Smith. Captain Harry Kirkwood, *Endeavour's* captain — who had also commanded her as the *John Biscoe* and recommended her to the New Zealand government — was somewhere ashore.

Bill, I learned later, had been awarded won a DSO as navigator of a midget submarine that attacked and sank the Japanese cruiser *Takao* in Johore Strait near the end of the war. And, as I've mentioned, he had already been down to McMurdo Sound the previous summer as a member of the advance party seeking out possible sites for Scott Base.

Endeavour had to feel her way cautiously through the pack ice once we reached the Southern Ocean.

The following day, several hundred relatives and friends were on hand to farewell us as we sailed at full tide — so that *Endeavour* rode above the wharf — following an official farewell by the Governor-General, Deputy Prime Minister and assorted political and civic dignitaries. Rolling steadily, we travelled overnight to Lyttelton, the port of Christchurch, for another civic reception and to meet the Duke of Edinburgh. He had arrived in the royal yacht *Britannia* from Melbourne, where he had been attending the 1956 Olympic Games, and was to accompany us as far as the pack ice before continuing around the Antarctic continent to the Atlantic and then home.

That evening all the expedition members were invited over to the *Britannia* for dinner, an informal but splendid affair which impressed me greatly. The flock of discreet waiters all look like and may well have been the younger sons of dukes, and a Royal Marine quintet played music in an anteroom throughout the meal. Other guests on board included several Antarctic veterans, such as Sir Raymond Priestley, a distinguished scientist who had been with both Scott and Shackleton. Several of us lingered over after-dinner drinks with these guests, asking all we could about this strange place called McMurdo Sound.

About midnight *Britannia* sailed off first and *Endeavour* followed, but not before a most unfortunate incident that, because I reported it fully as I was duty-bound to do, triggered off Captain Kirkwood's long-running and quite unpleasant feud with me about what should, and what he felt should not, be reported about his ship and crew.

On the stern of *Endeavour* was the expedition's Auster aircraft that had been equipped with floats and was to be used for reconnaissance flights once we reached McMurdo. While manoeuvring from the tight berth where *Endeavour* had been placed alongside another ship, one of the overhanging wings of the Auster — yes, the *Endeavour* was that small! — smashed against the other ship, damaging the wing severely.

Fortunately, we were only sailing that night as far as Dunedin where our 35 huskies and four small pups were waiting to be loaded on board after being brought down from our training area in the Southern Alps. Aviation mechanics from a nearby air-force base boarded, removed the wing and took it off for repairs.

We stayed an extra night in Dunedin enjoying, I've got to confess, the generous hospitality of its citizens along with another civic reception, while waiting for a newly repaired wing. But next day the news was not good — it would take a couple of weeks to replace, so the good wing was also removed and stored for protection (all of which I fully reported) and we then made the short trip to New Zealand's most southern port, Bluff, where there was yet another civic reception, and a cargo of mutton to be loaded to feed the huskies. The repaired wing was flown down to McMurdo by a United States Navy Globemaster and was waiting for us when *Endeavour* arrived.

If all these civic receptions sound rather over the top, it has to be recalled that — I'm embarrassed to say — we were regarded, rather prematurely, as heroes by most New Zealanders. The Antarctic was still a remote, almost unknown place in those days and we were following in the steps of Scott! Everywhere we went we were besieged for autographs — I wonder what has happened to them all.

Finally, on 21 December, we steamed out of Bluff and were on our way, with most of us gradually adapting to *Endeavour's* rolling ways.

I should have mentioned one of the early, almost disastrous, results of this drunk-like roll, which occurred as we were leaving Wellington Harbour. Once outside the heads we hit a formidable swell and experienced for the first time the roll's full effect in open sea, made worse when the ship had to heave-to when part of its rigging snapped and repairs needed to be made — only the first of numerous small incidents that beset *Endeavour* had on our way south, I'm sorry to report. We should have been forewarned: *Endeavour* had leaked badly while being delivered to New Zealand, destroying a large quantity of expedition supplies in its holds.

The official account of the expedition mentions that shortly after the rigging repairs were made, expedition members noticed smoke coming from a pile of kitbags still stacked around the port winch that was situated immediately above the fully loaded magazine carrying explosives needed to blast foundations for Scott Base. What had happened, but was not mentioned to the captain or crew, was that one of our seasick colleagues had grabbed the winch starting-lever for support and had somehow managed to short-circuit the winch motor, causing the fire.

Now, after leaving Bluff and sailing south in reasonably sunny weather, occasionally interrupted by bleak overcast spells with rain, we soon settled into our routines, which included feeding the huskies and cleaning out their pens and swotting up on our duties for when we reached the continent.

During Christmas Eve we were puzzled, rather than alarmed, to learn that an unidentified ship had been picked up on radar crossing our bows, but the reason soon became clear when an increasingly strong and most unpleasant smell drifted up on the southern wind. The next day we came upon a huge Japanese whaling-fleet mother-ship, busy hauling in dead whales and butchering them. Christmas Day itself came and went with a brief service on deck because we wanted to push on until we reached the ice.

Two Royal New Zealand Navy frigates, *Pukaki* and *Hawera*, which had been escorting *Britannia* on her way east, had rejoined *Endeavour* before Christmas, steaming abreast but slightly behind us

and making wide S turns in order to slow down to *Endeavour*'s cruising speed.

Two days after Christmas, when small icebergs accompanied by sizeable chunks of loose ice began appearing in the sea, they left, taking with them our last letters home. Their hulls were far too thin to take safely a direct hit from even a small piece of floating ice, let alone the largish bergy-bits — which is the name explorers use to describe chunks of ice about the size of a house. They left soon after we all crossed the Antarctic Circle, smack on midday, becoming — incredible as it sounds — the first British Commonwealth ships to do so since HMS *Challenger* in 1874.

We passed the time as budding explorers or mountaineers with time on their hands usually do: studying, reading, playing chess or card games and listening to lectures from those of our colleagues with some knowledge of what we were likely to encounter in a few days' time.

Expedition members breaking up an ice floe to supply Endeavour's *water storage tanks, which were running low. Drinking water had been rationed. Here Ed Hillary is catching ice thrown by Trevor Hatherton in the foreground.*

I spent a lot of time on deck with our scientists, identifying accompanying sea birds and attempting to photograph them, but my efforts turned out far less successfully than the Duke of Edinburgh's: he later published a book of Antarctic birds. Taking specimen samples of sea life from the ocean also filled some time. Once we got into the ice, the innumerable colours and variety of diatoms and plankton frozen into the ice, and the richness of life in the ocean, were amazing.

On 29 December we were deep in the ice pack and as *Endeavour* was finding the going tough it was decided to stop and officially celebrate Christmas Day in style with, as I recall, a quite sumptuous luncheon. Afterwards most of the expedition members clambered down on to the hard-pressed ice floes and stretched their legs. Some of us even organised an impromptu game of baseball.

Next day I again got into Captain Kirkwood's bad books by reporting, in what I thought was a chatty, colourful story, how we were faring and that he had stopped *Endeavour* alongside a very large and heavily hummocked ice floe to replenish the ship's dwindling water supplies. Expedition members and ship's crew got busy with picks, shovels and ice axes and soon two tonnes of ice were thrown aboard and melted.

Apparently I was not supposed to record, in the captain's view, that we all got a great deal of fun as well as some much-needed exercise, by hacking away on the ice floe. I soon got a message from an embarrassed ship's radio operator that the captain had instructed that my message was 'to be delayed' while the radio remained on standby for more important naval messages to be exchanged with Wellington.

Incensed, I talked to our two expedition radio operators, Peter Mulgrew and Ted Gawn. They had a word with Ed and a compromise was reached: all my messages from then on would be sent by them, rather than the navy!

By now we were pushing steadily through the last vestiges of the ice pack and had become quite accustomed to the continual growl the floes made as *Endeavour* ploughed past. Lying in our bunks at night, most of us found the steady scraping of the ice a few inches away on the other side of the hull quite soporific.

But the seas were getting rougher and what was left of the pack ice was heaving up in huge swells, signifying quite clearly that there was a big storm raging in the Ross Sea, further south. By New Year's Day most of us were wedged firmly in our bunks unwilling to move about any more than absolutely necessary and, except for an insufferable few, quite uninterested in food. The ship rolled alarmingly and nobody except essential crew moved about.

Two days later, when the storm had passed, I managed to join the living again and write about it:

Endeavour *began rolling heavily, even though the sea was still covered by the pack and by Tuesday the ship was gripped by the gale. At its height,* Endeavour *recorded a roll to port of 47 degrees from vertical. Sometimes the deck railings were under water.*

The huskies bore the full brunt as the waves broke across the ship but they stood up to it well and none were injured, even though a towering wave smashed half a dozen cages and stove in one end of the packing case containing our other aircraft, the RNZAF Beaver. Fortunately it was not damaged.

One dog, Dismal, got free from his cage and had to be rescued from the forecastle by George Marsh, our expedition doctor, who is in charge of the dogs, helped by Peter Mulgrew and Ron Balham. In the afternoon, a party led by Sir Edmund made the cages secure and gave each husky some meat and a drink.

I'd done it again, in Captain Kirkwood's eyes: *Drinking water has been rationed on* Endeavour [in spite of our efforts a few days earlier] *and it is forbidden to have showers or to wash clothes.*

Happily, the same day, 3 January, the storm gradually blew itself out as Mount Erebus came slowly up over the horizon, the 3800-metre snow-covered active volcano on the north edge of Ross Island that marks the entrance to McMurdo Sound.

We were almost there but *Endeavour* still had to force its way through thousands of tonnes of drifting sea ice, broken up and then packed in miles-long clumps by the storm.

Thick, jumbled sea ice finally halted *Endeavour* right at the entrance to the sound as it attempted to reach Butter Point, which had been initially chosen as the possible site of Scott Base on the western side of the sound, underneath the solid wall of the Royal Society Range.

Endeavour was further hampered in its ability to pick a safe route through the ice because of the damage to the Auster. As I've mentioned, it had been intended to lower the aircraft over the side of the ship once we reached McMurdo to make a reconnaissance whenever the ship's passage looked difficult.

Fortunately, the American ice-breaker *Glacier* was in McMurdo Sound, punching a very big channel, five kilometres wide at its entrance, in toward Hut Point, where the American base was being established on the eastern side. Coming to the rescue, as I told readers back home, the *Glacier* made short work of breaking a path for *Endeavour* and soon we were at a safe berth against solid ice, off Butter Point.

Our patchy relationship with Captain Kirkwood, RN

Captain Harry Kirkwood, OBE, DSC and Bar, RN, was reputed to be one of the most experienced British captains in ice conditions, but he barely tolerated the presence of rank and file members of our expedition or even, it seemed, most of his Royal New Zealand Navy officers and seamen.

He took a Queeg-like pleasure in making life difficult for ordinary expedition members. There may have been an explanation for this: I learned later that the navy had lobbied hard to be in charge of the whole New Zealand expedition, but this was firmly rebuffed by the government. And, of course, Kirkwood was a British naval captain in charge of a New Zealand crew whom he seemed to regard as inferior colonials!

The first major disagreement between Kirkwood and Ed Hillary flared up on 30 December. 'It was a hell of a row, actually,' Ed told us when he came down from the bridge shortly after lunch, looking furious.

The background was that from the time *Endeavour* reached the pack ice the ship had been stopping and starting for apparently no reason at all — and certainly no explanation was given — and after three days we had scarcely made any headway. Let me take up the account (with many epithets removed!) written at the time in my diary:

There's near mutiny among the expedition members at this stop-start lack of progress and that includes those among us who are navy types. How Ed stands it we don't know — but he hasn't much option; the captain is god on a navy ship.

Kirkwood will not let any of his officers steer the ship through the ice. Consequently we stop at night — 12 hours last night — while he gets sleep. And he shuts down the engines so that, with the southerly wind, we are drifting back during the night. The

midday plots for the past three days show this: 28 December, 68' 42' south, 179' 59' east; 29 December, 69' 22' south, 179' 40' east; 30 December, 69' 39' south, 179' 45' east.

Then he stops for any excuse during the day. This morning, for example, he stopped beside a large floe so that we could replenish the drinking water. Why he couldn't have done this during the night — there's no darkness — when we were stopped, none of us know. He won't even have a man in the crow's-nest to point out the leads.

The delay is potentially very serious indeed to the expedition. Every day lost now is two days at the end of summer. Some of the chaps have to make sledging journeys of up to 600 miles [960 km] before the onslaught of winter. We may not get the base completed in time if the weather is unkind — each hut cannot be assembled until there is a guarantee of at least 12 hours' fine weather.

As soon as the pack becomes at all dense he stops although we've got 14 inches [35.5 cm] of heart oak to take on the ice. He'll let the ship drift back for half an hour or so, then charge and, of course, the ice splits immediately. I asked one of the ship's engineers why Kirkwood didn't put the engines in reverse and he said, 'I'm damned if I know. The engines are here and he won't use them.'

I'm in a hell of a position as a newsman. I can't file a story without something to hang it on, even if I could get it past the captain's scrutiny. It's his word against ours and he, for the record anyway, has the experience. Kirkwood, according to Jim Spence, the ship's radio operator who has become a friend, is sending messages back to the navy in Wellington each day saying 'beset by ice', 'ice unnavigable' and so on. He'll probably get a decoration!

We have a number of very experienced Antarctic men in our expedition — Lieutenant Commander

This is the ladder, in need of repair and with rungs missing, that Captain Kirkwood ordered be hung over the bow — instead of a normal gang-plank — for expedition members to use to get on and off the ship.

Richard Brooke and Dr George Marsh from British expeditions and chaps like Ed, Bob Miller, John Claydon, Bernie Gunn, Trevor Hatherton and Harry Ayres who have been in these conditions before. To a man they are emphatic that Kirkwood is wrong in his judgement. George and Richard, who have sailed with Kirkwood before on the British side of Antarctica, say he has previously shown the same judgement, or lack of it. Our question is, does he lack elementary courage?

Last year, when I was discussing this with Ed while writing this book, he said, referring to his argument with Kirkwood: 'I thought I was being pretty circumspect, actually. Kirkwood gave me a real earful and snorted about "people who have been down this way only once before". In my diary, I noted at the time that Ed said Kirkwood complained that he had fools in his crew.

Fortunately, the next day the storm blew up, as I recount, and by the time the seas had quietened again the ice had dispersed and that problem was solved.

But later on, some of the rebellious Royal New Zealand Navy members of the crew told me that when *Endeavour* was berthed against the ice in McMurdo Sound, the only way for expedition members to board the ship, on Kirkwood's instructions, was up a broken rope ladder hanging from the bow. I believe it was intentionally made difficult for landlubbers like ourselves to climb.

I have recorded how I was immediately in his bad books by reporting adversely some of *Endeavour*'s earlier mishaps, and his dislike of me unfortunately was shared by two or three of his New Zealand officers who would mutter comments like 'watch out' whenever I passed by. Journalists must learn to have thick skins.

Yet Kirkwood seemed to be respected by the navy and had a long record of voyaging in the Southern Ocean, serving on the Royal research ship *Discovery II* for six years before the Second World War, visiting the Ross Sea on several occasions and twice circumnavigating the Antarctic continent — once in summer, and once in winter. He had been in command of *Endeavour* for several years when it was the *John Biscoe*.

Rear Admiral George Dufek, whom I felt honoured to call a friend, spoke highly of Kirkwood, calling him 'the best ice captain I had ever known in either of the Polar Regions. I was tremendously impressed by the way he handled his small ship in the ice. He and his crew did a fine job.'

Perhaps, in hindsight and to be charitable, it was just the Royal Navy's way.

Randal Heke, foreman in charge of building Scott Base, spent a lot of his time on the voyage south swotting up on detailed construction specifications. At 28, he already had an impressive career supervising projects in Western Samoa, Niue and the Chatham Islands for the Ministry of Works.

Bernie fell through the ice and Bob swung his camera case for Bernie to catch hold.

Suddenly the ice gave way under Bob, who fell through just as Bernie managed to struggle clear. This very shaky photograph, the last I took before trying to help them both, gives some idea, I hope, of what they experienced.

Bernie, Bob and I escape a serious wetting

When *Endeavour* first stopped alongside what looked to be a solid ice floe, about 40 metres by 60 metres, Bob Miller, Bernie Gunn and I got permission to go over the side to photograph the ship alone in the Southern Ocean. 'You know, intrepid stuff,' I remember saying to Ed at the time. I wrote later that night in my diary:

We climbed down a rope ladder and stepped one at a time on to a small floe, which didn't feel too safe, and from there to the larger floe, with a line-up of chaps hanging over the ship's side shouting cheerfully morbid remarks.

Bob and Bernie had been on floes before and they looked confident so I followed, happily enough. I'd just unslung my camera when one of my feet went right through the ice into the water. It gave me a bit of a jolt but I wasn't particularly worried because everyone who has been on floes says you do sometimes go through a bit, but under the top layer of ice is an older, harder layer that supports you.

I took a couple of photographs of *Endeavour* about 30 metres from the ship and then turned to shoot Bob, who was between Bernie and me, when I saw that Bernie had gone right through

the ice up to his chest in the bitterly cold sea and was hanging on desperately, up to his shoulders in the deathly water. I shouted to Bob, who turned and got to Bernie first, leaning forward to give him a hand.

As I said in my diary:

I thought everything was going to be okay, and began to photograph 'the rescue' — I guess the newsman in me — when quietly and without any noise at all the ice just disappeared beneath Bob and he was in the water too. They were about ten feet [three metres] away.

I was pretty scared but I knew I had to help and edged forward although Bob shouted at me to get back. Bernie managed to keep hold of a stronger piece of ice and slide on to it on his belly, undoubtedly helped by Bob while I grabbed Bob's camera strap, which he swung at me, and somehow, I don't quite know how, they were both beside me on the floe again.

We were still about 30 yards [27 m] from the ship and the floe was slowly breaking up all around us. Cautiously we started back, with our feet occasionally breaking through. We knew we had to keep fairly close together in case one of us fell in again.

To make matters worse, Endeavour *was slowly drifting back and only its bow was now against the ice. Johnny Douglas, the bosun, and Jack Hoffman, our explosives expert, were frantically untying the rope ladder which was now hanging over into the water and moving it up to the bow while we waited underneath.*

Bob was very wet and he went up first while Bernie and I held the bottom of the ladder, then Bernie held it for me. I'm a landlubber and found it hard work but it was a lot tougher climb for him with no one holding the bottom and he took a long time before Johnny and I could grab him and haul him the rest of the way.

Anyway, to shorten a long story, we went below, with everyone pretty subdued, had hot showers and hung our clothes to dry in the engine room. About half an hour later I went back on deck and the floe had drifted about 100 metres from us, split into three pieces right across the hole where Bernie had gone down. It was now clear the floe had been just rotten sea ice with a few inches of snow on top and no thick old ice below.

Endeavour *at its berth against the sea ice in McMurdo Sound.*

CHAPTER 4

DIGGING IN

For three days, advance parties with tractors and dog teams from *Endeavour*, which was now tied up to bay ice on the western side of McMurdo Sound, struggled without success to cross about 28 kilometres of jumbled sea ice, zigzagging back and forth to reach Butter Point — the chosen site to build Scott Base.

Soon after we arrived Ed Hillary and Bob Miller had flown over to Butter Point in one of the *Glacier*'s helicopters. Ed said later that the further they flew the further his spirits dropped. Although the planned site for the base was quite big enough, the difficulty was going to be how to get there.

At the foot of the Ferrar Glacier, off Butter Point, an iceberg 40 metres long barred the way. Beyond that was open water, about 300 metres wide, forming an impossible barrier. The western shore of McMurdo Sound was looking very inhospitable, although there appeared to be a possible alternative site on the Bowers Piedmont Glacier, to the south side of Butter Point.

Tractor parties led by Ed Hillary attempted to get around the humped ice barriers and melt pools, working their way slowly and painstakingly toward the rocky shore. They negotiated rough ice ridges forced up by pressure; slushy, melting pools and at one point a tidal crack about 1.8 metres wide. Anticipating such troubles, Ed had loaded heavy planks on his sledge and he and Peter Mulgrew managed to construct a bridge over which they edged the tractors.

By this time it was becoming obvious that even if a suitable beachhead was established it was going to be a tremendous problem to ferry some 900 tonnes of supplies to shore in order to build Scott Base and prepare for the coming winter.

While this probing by the advance party went on, some of us were also very busy unloading essential equipment off *Endeavour* on to the sea ice ready for transportation, while the rest got on with other chores, including exercising the huskies or hunting down a small pod of seals and then killing and preparing them as food for the dogs, who were delighted to finally get off the ship.

Soon afterwards, *Endeavour* left the temporary advance base and sailed for the United States Navy's Operation Deepfreeze base at Ross Island, on the eastern side of McMurdo where the Scott Base construction party had arrived on the American cargo ship, *Private John R Towle*, with the bulk of the prefabricated huts that were to become the expedition's home.

Our RNZAF pilots, Squadron Leader John Claydon and Flying Officer Bill Cranfield, were also busy searching for a suitable strip of glacier ice or flat shoreline from which to operate the Beaver and Auster and were not happy about what they saw: Butter Point and the Ferrar Glacier, which had seemed so suitable

Unloading sledging gear during an initial survey of Butter Point.

for our base during a reconnaissance the previous year, were not shaping up. 'It now seems,' I wrote, 'that none of the possible base sites on the western side of McMurdo Sound near the Ferrar Glacier can be occupied this summer because of transhipment difficulties.'

By 8 January 1957, Hillary knew that Butter Point had to be abandoned and was casting his mind over two or three alternative sites that had been previously marked out. Then John Claydon, who had sailed across the sound in *Endeavour*, called up by radio from the Operation Deepfreeze base to urge Ed to examine a site recommended by the Americans at Pram Point on the south shore of Ross Island, hard up against the Ross Ice Shelf.

Admiral George Dufek once more generously came to the rescue by sending a helicopter to pick up Ed and Bob, who had a long talk with him after making an aerial reconnaissance of Hut and Pram points. They then set off in a Ferguson tractor unloaded from *Endeavour* for a closer look and to test the feasibility of a supply route from ship to the base site.

Wasting no time, they travelled that evening, with the sun low in the southern sky. Ed had already decided that it was much safer, when exploring new territory, to travel during the 'night' hours (although the sun did not set) because it was colder and the ice was firmer.

Driving from *Endeavour* across the sea ice proved

Above: *Dog teams got valuable training and exercise helping unload* Endeavour.
Opposite: *Unloading* Endeavour *continued for three weeks without let-up, often driving over slushy, melting sea ice that — we hoped — was at least a metre thick.*

reasonably easy — there was a firm surface although there were what we were coming to accept as 'normal' tidal cracks and melt pools that proved as slushy as ever. They also encountered a problem that dogged us all for the next couple of months — churned-up areas with deep pools of water caused by the heavy American tractors that were used to smooth their airfield, which had been carved out of the bay ice.

I, for one, found that when driving a tractor I always negotiated these melt pools with my heart in my mouth, all too conscious that just below, hope-fully a metre or two below, were a couple of hundred metres of very cold water. One American had already been lost when his tractor crashed through thin ice, and another was also to be drowned only a few days after we began unloading *Endeavour*.

Past these obstacles, Ed and Bob found the way was rough but easily navigated. Better still, there was gentle access to the terraces on Pram Point, which turned out to be a low, rounded promontory to the south-east of Cape Armitage. The Ross Ice Shelf — a very deep, flat and safe surface — was only about half a kilometre from the point and led directly south toward the Pole. Pram Point itself was an ice-free, firm shingle surface about 15 metres above sea level.

John Claydon was confident that he could establish a good airstrip a short distance away and, just as importantly, there was a large seal rookery nearby, ensuring a steady supply of food for the huskies.

As a bonus, Scott Base inhabitants would have a magnificent view westward of the Royal Society Range with its row of peaks up to 3900 metres and also directly south to Black and White islands and Mount Discovery. Beyond was Minna Bluff and the route to the South Pole.

Behind, gently rising up from Cape Armitage was the awesome view of Mount Erebus, all 4010 metres, with its eternal stream of smoke billowing from the crater, and further west Mount Terror, 3260 metres, both named in 1840 for the ships in the Ross expedition.

'Really quite salubrious,' said Ed, using one of his favourite words at the time.

Pram Point was a historic spot, within a few kilometres of the areas where the British expeditions at the beginning of the 20th century had been based. Scott discovered and named Pram Point in 1902. That year all the sea ice had cleared out from McMurdo and it was necessary to use a praam — a type of Norwegian dinghy — to cross the open water to get to the Ross Ice Shelf.

Elated, Ed and Bob returned to *Endeavour* and arranged for the ship to sail back to Butter Point to recall the field parties. All of us were immediately set to work, to make up for lost time. Within a few hours, the construction party began surveying and levelling the terraces and a small tent camp, complete with a primitive cookhouse, was established.

Next evening, 10 January, the tractor trains began rolling, sledging supplies from *Endeavour* and the *Towle* to Pram Point, initially a 20-kilometre trip that

Early days of establishing Scott Base.

took two-and-a-half to three hours if all went well, which it quite often didn't. Later the distance shrank to about 12 kilometres as the sea ice continued, in the summer thaw, to break up and drift out to sea.

We worked two shifts, each supposed to be of about 12 hours, around the clock. All of us snatched sleep where we could: usually on *Endeavour* but often in a tent at Pram Point. Ed was everywhere, seemingly going without sleep for long periods.

For the next three weeks, in addition to my job of writing daily stories for the media back home, driving a tractor was my second most constant chore. There were occasional but welcome breaks, of course, to spend time with, and report on, the field parties, now heading south and west to find a safe route up to the Polar Plateau.

Within a few days we even had, believe it or not, a Scott Base post office! Arthur Helm, an enthusiastic student of the history of Antarctic exploration had, for several years previously, been honorary secretary of the New Zealand Antarctic Society and had suddenly found himself propelled into becoming secretary and general dogsbody of the newly formed Ross Sea Committee. In real life he was a historian and archivist at the post office and brought his job with him to the expedition. He even organised impromptu first-day covers during our voyage. (My daughters still hoard the letters and envelopes they received from me.) Once Scott Base was selected, Arthur lost no time setting up a post office inside a crate that had contained our Beaver aircraft.

Arthur had brought down in *Endeavour* a staggering 95,000 special first-day covers bought and posted by people back in New Zealand and, once Scott Base was completed, he was ruthless in

roping in those of us who had a spare moment to help stamp them. They were then taken back to New Zealand and put through the regular mail service. He also did brisk business with the Americans.

By 14 January, the kitchen, dining and radio huts were up at Scott Base, although (of necessity) only sketchily fitted out thanks to the way the prefabricated panels had been stored. The main radio mast was also up, with two other masts to follow. In all, there were six basic huts: four living and sleeping huts, one housing the generator that was also for sledge and tractor repairs, and one scientific laboratory. In addition, there were three smaller huts for seismology, geomagnetic and other scientific work.

Sergeant Wally Tarr and Corporal Peter Tate, RNZAF, whose constant hard work earned the respect of all of us as they made themselves virtually indispensable, had the Beaver aircraft assembled and flying one day later. Two days on, Buck Bucknell was turning out hot, sustaining meals from his kitchen.

But Ed Hillary had an even bigger problem nagging him.

George Marsh, leading one of the dog teams, had just reported that the Ferrar Glacier was proving quite unsuitable for dog travel and would be a very hard slog for tractors, assuming they could first reach the area.

How, then, to find a practical route through the mountains and up on to the plateau?

Boarding the newly test-flown Beaver, Ed flew over to the region of the Ferrar Glacier to try to find a way up through the mountain barrier but he eventually had to admit defeat. There was just no suitable sledging route there.

Ed then remembered that Bernie Gunn, our geologist who was also a skilled mountaineer, had reported seeing the Skelton Glacier 200 kilometres or so south of Ross Island during an aerial reconnaissance while visiting McMurdo the

previous summer, and reported that it appeared to offer possible access through the mountains.

Two days later, with the Beaver settling in nicely, Bill Cranfield flew Ed, Bob, George Marsh and Richard Brooke, a surveyor and a lieutenant commander in the Royal Navy, down to the Skelton to have a look. George and Richard, both Englishmen, had been selected by Fuchs to be with the New Zealand party.

It is no exaggeration to say they were stunned by what they saw. This was the way to go!

I vividly remember their enthusiasm upon their return. Ed later wrote:

The lower part of the glacier seemed straightforward and easy . . . about 40 miles up [64 km] *we came to a much steeper rise. To the left was a great icefall, but long snow slopes led out under Mount Huggins and although these were peppered with crevasses it did look as if a zigzag route through them would lead to the enormous snowfields at the head of the glacier. As we flew on up through this magnificent area with its great mountains and spectacular glaciers, and as the route unfolded beneath us our enthusiasm grew. It is often difficult from an aircraft to judge accurately . . . but this glacier appeared to offer excellent prospects for success.*

Running short of fuel, they returned to Scott Base but only two hours later they were airborne again, this time with John Claydon as pilot, and flying at about 2400 metres through the mountains they reached the Polar Plateau itself and the head of the Skelton Glacier. The route to the South Pole had been found.

Wasting no time, the following evening three dog teams set off across the Ross Ice Shelf for a ground

Early construction of Scott Base
Far left: *The construction crew lived in tents, preparing the site, while we ferried prefabricated building panels, stores and equipment from Endeavour.*
Left: *The mess hut, erected within the first four days, was a welcome haven for a quick hot drink.*

Faced with more delays in proving a route up to the Polar Plateau, Ed decided to recall the other dog teams and fly them directly to the Skelton. This would mean postponing the task of proving the route over the ice shelf to the Skelton, a necessary task later completed by Bob Miller and Roy Carlyon, another surveyor. Neither had much previous experience with dog teams but both found the task so enjoyable they accomplished long sledging surveys the following year.

Ed and John immediately flew over to the Skelton in the Beaver and after a series of hair-raising attempts to land, which they recounted vividly upon their return, set down safely at the foot of the glacier. This was where a large depot would be established, serving both the New Zealand reconnaissance parties and, the following year, the tractor parties led by Hillary and Fuchs. It was one hour's flying from Scott Base and about 290 kilometres by land — at least a week's run by dog teams.

Within a few hours, Richard Brooke and Murray Ellis, one of our two engineers and a keen mountaineer, were flown in with a tent and food to establish what became known as the Skelton Depot. During the next two days the Beaver flew in 18 dogs, accompanied by Harry Ayres and Murray Douglas, both highly skilled Southern Alps guides, plus sledges, food and so on. But no radios: they

survey, driven by Richard, George, Harry Ayres and Peter Mulgrew. It was going to take them about a week to reach the foot of the Skelton.

Soon afterwards, on 20 January — exactly one year, as it turned out, before we were to greet Fuchs's party at the South Pole — the New Zealand flag was formally raised at Scott Base on the chipped, weather-beaten mast originally brought to McMurdo Sound by Scott during his 1902–04 expedition. It had been found lying in the snow near his base at Hut Point. The function was attended by Admiral Dufek and senior Americans.

By unanimous choice, the flag was raised by Randal Heke, who was in charge of the construction team and a great grandson of Hone Heke, the defiant Maori chief who repeatedly cut down the flagpole erected at Russell, the first capital of the fledgling New Zealand colony in 1840.

But, alas, very little was really going to plan and on the following day there was more bad news. Peter and Richard returned unexpectedly, covering about 50 kilometres with the dogs in one run, bringing the news that George Marsh, our doctor, had become ill.

If their returning without warning sounds strange, remember that radio reception was extremely unreliable. Our Beaver flew out and George was immediately evacuated by air to the American hospital, where there was great consternation when he was diagnosed with diphtheria, then a highly contagious and serious throat illness. For the rest of us, this meant a big step up in hygiene, both personally and, particularly, in the kitchen and bathrooms.

were still proving very unsatisfactory and too heavy to lug around.

A few days later, I saw the Skelton for myself. Because the field parties lacked reliable radio contact, our aircraft, which were flying in drums of diesel fuel, supplies of human and dog food and other equipment to Skelton Depot, also made regular flights up the glacier to check their progress.

With Bill Cranfield I made several of these trips, flying up the glacier to land beside the field team's tents to unload supplies and have a chat about progress. Usually Bill liked to divert through the lower mountain ranges on the way back to Scott Base, taking photographs and generally getting to know a region that had never before been seen by humans.

On one occasion I confessed to Bill that my bladder was uncomfortably full. 'I know just the spot,' he yelled over the Auster's engine and soon we were standing on a smooth snow surface in a small valley some distance up the glacier. 'Ed and I had to do this last week,' Bill said. 'I've been keeping an eye out for convenient places [that's Bill's pun, not mine] ever since.'

I insisted on taking the temperature — which meant swinging the gauge on a rope around my head to get an accurate reading — and found that it was just minus 20°C.

Back in New Zealand a year or two later, when some of us were roped in to address luncheon clubs about our exploits, I usually got a laugh when recounting this story — and had to answer the inevitable question by reassuring my largely male audience that, no, we didn't get frostbite and even at that temperature, on a sunny day there was no discomfort at all.

Above: *Our modest flag-raising after completing the first hut preceded the official naming of Scott Base two weeks later on 20 January.*

Right: *The original and newly completed Scott Base, looking south across the Ross Ice Shelf toward the Pole. The seven buildings were connected by a tunnel walkway that was covered by drifting snow in winter. The mess hut is in the centre, with living and sleeping quarters to the right.*

Scott Base 'built to last 100 years'

Scott Base was a model of compactness. The six main huts were linked by covered walkways giving the inhabitants easy access between buildings without the necessity to put on protective clothing, even during winter blizzards. Made of curved corrugated iron, the covered ways were tied down by steel cables and lined with tins, boxes and packages of food and other equipment.

New Zealand's Ministry of Works architects had boasted that Scott Base 'would last 100 years'. The prefabricated walls of the huts resembled refrigerators, except that they were designed to keep the cold out — insulated against minus 100° of frost — about minus 50°C — and built to withstand winds of more than 160 kilometres per hour.

Behind the main huts, climbing the gentle slope, were the radio and smaller scientific masts and three small scientific huts. I spent a couple of fascinating days late in January helping Jack Hoffman, our explosives expert, erect the main radio, and some other, masts. Anchoring the mast, Jack showed me, was relatively easy after we had hauled it up. We just drilled deep holes into the permafrost on Pram Point, inserted the stays, and then poured water into the holes. It set hard instantly, firmer than concrete.

Ted Gawn and Peter Mulgrew, our two radio operators, were soon hard at work attempting to establish permanent contact with New Zealand. On 1 February, our radio link was up and running and Ed sent the first telegram — to his wife Louise, back in Auckland.

From then on, Scott Base was able to maintain regular daily radio schedules with New Zealand and all of us were able to send occasional brief messages home. Five weeks later, on 5 March, Scott Base made contact with Shackleton Base, enabling Ed and Fuchs to talk directly to each other for the first time since arriving in the Antarctic.

On one wall of the main mess hall at Scott Base was a large painting of New Zealand rural mountain country in spring, depicting a slouch-hatted shepherd with his horse and dogs herding a flock of sheep and their lambs running through the tussock. It made a fine contrast to the scene outside.

Colour ran riot in the bedrooms from a large stock of paint, pretty much to individual choice. The sleeping huts were cleverly arranged so that each man had, in effect, a single room. To achieve this, the double-tiered bunks were placed in the centre of partitioned rooms. Then the space along the side of the top bunk was closed off and the opposite side closed on the lower bunk. This gave each L-shaped room its own window, with a writing table underneath.

Meanwhile, over at Shackleton, they too were digging in

A small base at Shackleton had been established the previous summer, 1955–56, and by early January 1957, just about the same time that Ed had decided upon Pram Point for the site of Scott Base, Vivian Fuchs and his team who had sailed from England reached Shackleton, also aided by both ice-breaker and aircraft. They were welcomed by a small group that had wintered over.

Their task, apart from building a more roomy base and stocking and equipping it for the coming winter, was to establish an advance station, about 480 kilometres out, which would be the jumping-off spot for the crossing of the Antarctic, one year hence.

Earlier reconnaissance flights had hinted that a land route south from Shackleton was not going to be easy to find and so Fuchs used an Otter, an aircraft which was our Beaver's big brother, to make reconnaissances. They also, like us, had a Beaver and an Auster for shorter trips.

By 5 February, Fuchs had decided to build a hut at South Ice, as the advance station was eventually called, just past a number of formidable barriers — a good many crevasses, a large chasm that extended for 50 to 65 kilometres and an equally daunting ice wall at least 100 kilometres long that would push their land route into the Shackleton ranges and across the foot of two small glaciers.

They had a wretched time establishing South Ice, flying as regularly as they could from Shackleton but often being forced to turn back because of bad weather. In addition they spent a week early in March searching for and finally managing to rescue two scientists in the party who had been surveying the Whichaway Nunataks nearby and had been unable to move from their tent because of a series of blizzards that had blown up from nowhere.

On 25 March, with the temperature already down to minus 40°C, Hal Lister, a glaciologist, Ken Blaiklock, a surveyor, and Jon Stephenson, an Australian geologist, were left at South Ice to face a bleak, windy, seven months of isolation during the Antarctic winter. They would not see their companions again until 8 October.

Their hut was a lightweight aluminium and plywood affair, buried into the snow for warmth. They had 15 tonnes of food and fuel, along with a generator that could also be driven by the wind.

During the winter night they made several sorties for scientific research and lived remarkably well.

At Shackleton, a much smaller and more basic base than Scott, Fuchs and his main party were also preparing for a long winter in conditions far less pleasant than at McMurdo. But they did have warm, comfortable living quarters that would, by design, be almost buried by snow storms. They had a large living room lined with books, off which were a kitchen, radio room, sleeping quarters, bathroom, a workshop, a surgery and a scientific area.

There was one interesting difference between Shackleton and Scott Bases. At Shackleton, a portrait of the Queen, who was the Commonwealth Trans-Antarctic Expedition's patron, hung in the mess hall. At Scott, there was a photograph of Robert Falcon Scott, resplendent in naval officer's uniform.

Right: *Pam knitted this orange sweater for me 'so that I wouldn't get lost' in the Antarctic. It was certainly far brighter than the much more sober clothes we normally wore around Scott Base.*
Left: *Piles of supplies at the Scott Base site.*

CHAPTER 5

The 'little workhorses'

Flying in often appalling conditions and frequently at high altitudes in extremely cold weather, the trans-Antarctic expedition's single-engine Otter, Beaver and Auster aircraft were the tireless workhorses that contributed mightily to the success of the crossing. Thanks to loving care from their mechanics they seldom faltered and there was never a serious mechanical difficulty or forced landing.

In use in the Antarctic over a period of some 16 months for reconnaissance, ferrying expedition members and huskies back and forth into the mountains and on to the Polar Plateau and — their most important task of all — lugging the fuel, food and other supplies needed to stock the depots that provided vital logistic support for the crossing parties, as well as to re-provision the men and dog teams on survey and geological missions.

In January 1958, toward the end of the expedition, the Otter used by Fuchs's team made the first single-engined crossing of the continent. They also had an Auster that was left at Shackleton.

The New Zealanders had a Beaver and an Auster. Both the New Zealand aircraft flew thousands of miles over hundreds of hours, back and forth, from Scott Field — the snow strip at Scott Base — up on to the Polar Plateau, as well as far south across the Ross Ice Shelf and around McMurdo Sound.

The Otter and Beaver were made by deHavilland Aircraft Corporation of Canada and had been well tested in the Arctic, while the Auster came from the Auster Aircraft Company in England. All were modified for Antarctic conditions including being fitted with skis and also, in the case of the Austers, floats. They had special radio transmitters, radio beacons and radar, and mysterious equipment called Bendix polar-path compass and gyro systems.

Both the deHavilland aircraft had Pratt & Whitney Wasp air-cooled radial supercharged engines, the Otter's rated at 600 hp and the Beaver's at 450 hp. The Auster's engine was a Gipsy Major air-cooled, inverted inline of 145 hp. The lighter Beaver had a slightly better performance than its big brother, with a cruising speed of about 230 kph, compared to 205 kph, and a service ceiling of 5400 metres compared to the Otter's 5220 metres. The tough little Auster cruised at a shade over 160 kph and struggled to reach 3150 metres.

Left: *I'm helping Squadron Leader John Claydon, RNZAF, our chief pilot, load camping gear into the New Zealand Auster for a trip into the mountains. In summer, all work on the aircraft was done in the open air in usually fine and always completely dry weather.*

Loading a husky into our Beaver for a trip into the mountains.

The small vessel dwarfed between two large American cargo ships in the top right of the picture is
Endeavour, *emphasising better than words just how compact our New Zealand expedition was.*

We called it 'Suicide Alley'

We called it 'Suicide Alley' and those of us who drove tractor trains along it every day agreed that as a highway it had nothing to commend it.

The 20-kilometre track, quite tortuous most of the time, snaked over melting ice floes from where *Endeavour* was moored against the edge of the sea ice in McMurdo Sound to our site for Scott Base, at Pram Point on the southern tip of Ross Island, facing the Ross Ice Shelf.

But to those of us who had been conscripted as tractor drivers — biologists, geologists and surveyors, as well as myself — it had become as familiar as the road home as we drove back and forth, unloading the ship. We knew every changing tidal crack in the ice, every slushy patch needing caution. Often the tractors and Weasels — a type of tracked jeep — sank up to their wheel hubs in melted icy water; occasionally their exhausts burbled away beneath the water's surface.

We prayed for the weather to stay overcast: bad weather that gave us nice, cold, sub-zero temperatures that would harden the track and make it safer. Unfortunately, clear blue skies with a warming sun persisted. So warm, in fact, that I sometimes drove wearing just a string singlet and good New Zealand-wool shirt. An anorak was always close by, though, in case a chill wind sprang up.

Our task, stretching over about three weeks, was to navigate our trusty and hard-working Ferguson tractors while towing sledges laden with prefabricated sections of the huts that would grow into the base village. There were also crates, crates and more crates of food, equipment and fuel that would last the expedition for 18 months.

A round trip could take as long as five or six hours. More if, as frequently happened, we had trouble with the tractors' still experimental metal tracks. In the first week, as we raced to get Scott Base established, it was quite common to work 20 hours non-stop.

At first the road from the ship was a winding, rather hair-raising, route dipping through melt holes and past blue, broken cracks where the ice was beginning to break up in the summer heat.

We, the drivers and our occasional passengers, were always conscious that about a metre below — at least we hoped it was a metre below but it often turned out to be much less — was the deadly cold, green water of McMurdo Sound. The water was so cold that it could kill within minutes. Soon, however, there was a tendency to become hardened to the conditions, to accept them without much thought. Or there was, until Roy Carlyon saw a seal poking its head out of a melt hole right beside the trail, and realised the hole must go right through.

Some of the year's supplies waiting to be stored away.

We always drove in convoys of at least two tractors so that we could help each other when — and it was often — required. Frequently one tractor driver would walk ahead on the softer stretches with an ice axe, testing the surface.

After a week or so, some Americans arrived from their base to service two of their cargo ships that had just arrived, and they bulldozed the snow and ice into a smoother, if not safer, surface. That took something of the tenseness out of the first four or five kilometres, so much so that on one trip I was startled to see Murray Douglas bowling slowly toward me, all alone in a Weasel, sound asleep, with his pipe clenched firmly between his teeth. Before I was able to reach him, the Weasel bumped into the piled snow beside the track and fortunately woke him up.

The next three or four kilometres retained some of the former hazards of suicide alley, mainly because it was criss-crossed by fuel lines to the air strip which had been bulldozed out of much firmer, thicker sea ice nearer land. Black fuel lines have a habit of melting wide crevasses into white snow and ice. There were, too, gaping tidal cracks to trap a vehicle. Sometimes cargoes on the sledges would be awash as we drove through.

But it was around Cape Armitage, the last long stretch to Scott Base, that prompted Trevor Hatherton, our chief scientist, to compare tractor driving with playing Russian roulette: 'Sooner or later you're bound to cop it!'

A couple of days after he said that a Weasel carrying himself, Ed Hillary and Peter Mulgrew crashed through and was only stopped from plunging into about 250 metres of very cold water because the sledge it was towing ran on and wedged the Weasel in the hole.

The three escaped with nothing worse than a dunking when the vehicle sank until its cab was awash. They managed to get out quickly because Hillary had ordered that the hoods be taken off the cabs after an American Weasel had sunk in similar circumstances the previous week, drowning one man.

'The Weasel's buoyancy tanks helped hold her,' Ed said and I later reported, 'but we certainly didn't waste any time getting out of there.' It took about five hours to drag the vehicle free and rescue the cargo.

Later the weather became more unstable. Once, when a storm was blowing up and the temperature was about minus 8°C, I cut my hand while fixing one of the track links that had an annoying habit of coming unstuck. The blood froze instantly on the metal surface, like red enamel.

The work of unloading the ship ended during the last week of January, and not a day too soon. By then most of the bay ice was thawing rapidly and breaking off in half-mile slabs before drifting into the Ross Sea where it would eventually form the nucleus of next year's pack ice.

We had hauled more than 1000 tonnes from *Endeavour* and the *Towle* — not only the prefabricated huts but, according to a story I wrote, about 12,000 different items ranging from a piano to a barrel of pickled pork (donated by an Auckland businessman) and even pipe cleaners. Only 10 of the 23 men wintering over smoked, but two were pipe smokers.

I remember Ed and Bob poring over pages of foolscap lists in Auckland three months before we sailed. The list began with 'adzes, awls, axes', and had everything anyone could think of, including a boot maker's last, tailors' thimbles, vaseline for cracked lips and dubbin for cracked boots along with a range of metal and woodworking tools for budding handymen.

There were such daunting items as sheath knives and firearms, along with felt slippers, electric toasters and Dramamine tablets, which anticipated our rough trip south in *Endeavour*. Of course there were all the essential items, but also, in addition to the

piano, there were mouth organs, footballs, cricket gear, playing cards and many board games including chess and draughts sets.

We installed the large record player with 500 long-playing records in the mess hall and created a library of about 750 books. Time would not drag during the long winter months.

Now everything was ashore, and the real work of Scott Base, both scientific and exploratory, could begin in earnest.

Above: *Huskies tethered for the night.*
Left: *Cracks like this constantly appeared in the melting sea ice that we drove across every day.*

CHAPTER 7

VISITING THE OLD HUTS OF SCOTT AND SHACKLETON

When the initial construction of Scott Base was almost completed, a small group of us took a brief break to visit Nimrod Hut at Cape Royds, about 32 kilometres north from Scott Base. It is named after the ship that carried Shackleton's 1907–09 expedition, during which he ascended the Beardmore Glacier and got to within 139 kilometres of the Pole before turning back when bad weather, combined with dwindling food and fuel, threatened their safe return.

Later a few of us also visited Cape Evans, 18 kilometres or so north of our base and the site of the hut built by Scott as the jumping-off point for his ill-fated journey to the South Pole in 1909–12.

In all, a scatter of five bases lie under Mount Erebus along the western shores of Ross Island, testimony to the reasonably safe anchorage and easy land access of that part of McMurdo Sound. There are also a couple of early huts and more recent bases to the north-west, across the Ross Sea on the Antarctic coast called Victoria Land dating back to 1899, with no direct access to the continent because of formidable coastlines and glaciers.

Amundsen, knowing that Scott would be in residence in McMurdo Sound in 1910, built a temporary base, Framheim, on the Ross Ice Shelf much further to the east of Ross Island for his successful dash to the Pole in 1911.

In 1956 when we arrived, there was ample evidence around the old huts of unpublicised visits during the past decades when others had landed, undoubtedly whalers who did not advertise their presence for commercial reasons.

Scott's first hut, called Discovery Hut after the ship that carried his team there, was built near Pram Point for the 1902–04 expedition and is now sandwiched between the Americans' Williams Air Operating Facility (now McMurdo Station) and New Zealand's Scott Base, opened in 1957. The Williams Air Operating Facility, established in 1955, was named after driver third-class Richard T Williams, who is the first American killed there when the tractor he was driving crashed through the bay ice.

When we first arrived in McMurdo Sound, the Discovery Hut was still largely as it had been left by the earlier explorers, partly filled with ice and snow. Venturing in, I found myself in what had been the laboratory of the expedition photographer, H G Ponting. Scattered around were unused photographic plates and mouldy bottles of the chemicals he used. Discovery Hut has since been cleared of snow, tidied up, and is now a venerated historic monument, preserved and given tender loving care by official visitors on recreational tours each summer.

Hillary says he saw Shackleton's ghost

Ed Hillary, normally the most pragmatic of individuals, who visited the Nimrod Hut a few weeks after us, told *The New Zealand Herald* years later that he met Shackleton's ghost there.

'I'm not a person who sees things very much,' he said, 'but when I opened the door I distinctly saw Shackleton walking towards me and welcoming me. It's the only time I can ever remember something like that so I have a very warm feeling indeed for Shackleton and for his hut. I really believe Shackleton's hut must be preserved.'

Left: *We found this motor sledge, used by Scott's expedition with limited success, at Cape Evans. It is now back in New Zealand. Examining it are Derek Wright, our cinematographer (left), Dick Barwick, biologist (centre) and Ron Balham, biologist and meteorologist (right).*

Shackleton, who had been on Scott's 1902–04 expedition, had been forced to stay at Cape Royds rather than use the Discovery Hut after he had been warned off by Scott who, in the manner of explorers those days, maintained he had first rights to McMurdo Sound. Shackleton apparently endeavoured to heed Scott's demands but found it impossible to find a suitable landing at his first choice along King Edward VII Land near where Amundsen was to establish his temporary base.

Cape Royds is home to an Adélie penguin rookery that, when we were there, had an adult population of about 2000. Because it was mid-summer when we visited, the rookery was crowded with downy young penguins who, along with their parents, took a very inquisitive look at us. There is also a big skua colony nearby — they're aggressive gulls that, nature being the way nature is, prey on nesting penguins, scaring them off their eggs by dive-bombing tactics then eating the eggs or picking off abandoned babies.

They dive bombed us too, swooping unnervingly near our heads.

Nimrod Hut lies in a very sheltered position in a small bay, really the hollow of a volcanic arm, at the foot of Mount Erebus and there were only small patches of icy snow over the rocky volcanic ash, still melting in the summer sunshine. It had cramped living quarters for 14 men as well as the remains of dog kennels, stables for the ponies, a meteorological station and a small laboratory.

The hut — listed on the World Monument Fund's 100 most endangered sites — is about 12 metres by 6 metres and had cables criss-crossed over the roof to anchor it against the harsh winter winds. It is set well back from the sea, over undulating ground, and was remarkably well preserved although the winds had bleached its wooden walls.

Williams Air Operating Facility at Hut Point. Scott Base is a couple of kilometres around to the right.

Dismay at state of historic huts

Dismayed at the state of the three historic huts erected in the first decade of the 20th century by the Scott and Shackleton expeditions, I wrote a feature article for the New Zealand Press Association that was widely published, suggesting that the National Historic Places Trust could take an interest.

New Zealanders with the trans-Antarctic expedition had been appalled by the neglect and their concern was echoed by high-ranking United States officers. We were willing to spend a few days shovelling snow and ice out of the huts and cleaning them up (and we did when time allowed) but official action was needed to make our work of lasting value.

The article sparked a flurry of letters to newspapers from concerned New Zealanders but the initial reaction from the Historic Places Trust

people was to say it would have to be determined whether the Ross Sea Dependency was covered by the Historic Places Trust Act, 1954. Happily, the chairman of the Ross Sea Committee, C M Bowden, was also chairman of the trust, so the creaking wheels of officialdom began to move.

Admiral George Dufek was not so slow: he had already ordered that his men were not to visit the huts except under the supervision of a ranking officer and were not to take souvenirs. He offered to join New Zealanders in tidying up although he was reluctant to do anything officially in case it was seen to be intruding upon British feelings and New Zealand territorial claims.

Scott's two huts at Cape Evans and Hut Point, I wrote, all showed signs of pillaging and were in a filthy condition. Food and rubbish lay around all the rooms to which access could be gained and opened film packs and empty beer cans were scattered about. Some of the mess was quite recent.

I described a photograph that had been taken inside the Cape Evans hut the previous year that showed the mess table set with plates and some tableware. When we visited, the table was strewn with opened tins of old expedition food, litter and articles from the surrounding shelves.

Shackleton's hut at Cape Royds was the best preserved and tidiest hut, probably because of its position. Hut Point, close to the American and Scott bases, was the most accessible to all visitors and a small amount of litter lay about, much of it from previous expeditions. The hut was almost completely filled with snow and ice which was probably a blessing in that it prevented access.

I quoted the famous French Arctic and Antarctic explorer, Paul Emile Victor, who visited the huts with us and suggested they should be preserved as places of historic interest. He agreed with our general feelings that no attempt should be made to transport the huts or their contents back to museums.

Fortunately, New Zealand authorities, including the Historic Places Trust, quickly sprang into action and for the past 50 years there have been regular summer visits, cleaning, tidying, preserving and forensically studying these fascinating historic sites. Controversially, there are some museums in New Zealand and elsewhere that do hold items from the huts.

Above left: *Scott's hut at Cape Evans, with remains of stores scattered about.*
Above right: *Ron Barwick, the author, Ron Balham, Derek Wright and Arthur Helm, secretary of the Ross Sea Committee, in front of Nimrod Hut.*

A friend at the time, Saul Pett, a reporter from American Associated Press, told me that when he had visited Nimrod Hut the previous year they found the entrance half-blocked by years of drifting snow 'although we could wriggle through'. They cleared the door but left the hut much as they found it. Most of the hut's glass windows were intact, but two had broken, allowing snow and slush to get in. We also cleared out the accumulated snow and ice that had come in the broken windows, wrote a note describing our visit and pinned it to the wall. Like Discovery Hut, it is now carefully looked after.

Like Pett and his companions, we found sleeping bags still lying about inside and, on the wall, a well-preserved photograph of King Edward and Queen Alexandra with a list of names below — mostly of Americans who visited in 1947. There was also a note, dated 1917, from the British relief party that had been a back-up to Shackleton's disastrous attempt to cross the continent. Oddly, there was

almost no furniture. Boxes of food marked 'British Antarctic Expedition 1908', some opened and the contents scattered about, lay around just as they had at Cape Evans. There was no sign of the Arroll Johnstone motor car Shackleton had experimented with as a means of pulling sledges. Presumably it had been taken back to England.

The Arroll Johnstone had a specially designed air-cooled, four-cylinder engine of about 15 hp that used exhaust gasses to keep the carburettor warm. It had been supplied by William Beardmore, a Scottish industrialist and one of Shackleton's patrons. In gratitude, Shackleton named the huge Beardmore Glacier, which he discovered and both he and Scott later used to reach the Polar Plateau, after the industrialist.

Large piles of equipment and boxes, some opened and others chewed open by skuas, lay about in great disorder. Some contained food that had been preserved in a perpetual deep-freeze for more than

40 years and was quite edible. Here there was also evidence of earlier visitors who had probably broken into boxes and removed food.

I remember finding one box labelled 'Tate & Lyle Sugar' that contained neatly packed smaller paper packages. We opened some and were amazed that each little square of sugar was perfectly preserved, presumably because of the extremely dry Antarctic atmosphere. There were other boxes marked 'Mayfair Pate' which turned out to be tins of bully beef, and stores of hams and marrow fat, tins of corn, raspberries and other fruit and a range of soups including mock turtle! The tins had each been coated to keep them airtight in what looked like red lead paint.

Later, at Scott's Cape Evans hut, the evidence seemed to indicate that his men, sadly leaving their leader and his four companions dead on the Ross Ice Shelf, had simply shut the hut's door and abandoned the base when it came time to leave. The hut is much closer to the bay, reached by a shallow, gravel beach. Broken equipment and packages of food also lay about.

It is a much larger hut, built on British Navy lines with separate messes and sleeping quarters for the officers and men, and so on. The hut was a dreadful mess, filled with ice and snow and we could only get into the galley by climbing up the porch. It has since been thoroughly cleaned up.

There were no penguins, just a lone seal and some skuas over by a large melt-pool about 40 metres from the hut. Beyond the hut on a small rise was a wooden cross and I climbed up for a look but there

Above left: *Scott's first hut, at Hut Point. Observation Hill is in the background.*
Top right: *Scott's hut at Cape Evans with* Endeavour *anchored in the bay.*
Lower right: *Looking down on Shackleton's hut at Cape Royds.*

appeared to be no inscription.

Sadly, we came across span lines where their huskies had been kept and found the intact skeletons of two dogs, still with collars and heavy chains around their necks — the cartilage and bones had frozen, holding the skeletons together. There were also scattered dog bones on a patch of rocky ground a few yards from the hut that the skuas had picked over. Leather straps used to harness the ponies, employed unsuccessfully to drag sledges, also lay around, but there was no sign of pony skeletons.

The remains of a rusting iron motor sledge were nearby, the last of three 'caterpillar-tractor sledges' (as they were sometimes called) that Scott took south after testing them in Norway and Switzerland, hoping they would eventually replace huskies and ponies. He had been trying to improve on Shackleton's experiment three years earlier with the Arroll Johnstone motor car.

Scott's motor sledges were moderately successful on good, flat surfaces, hauling up to two-and-a-half tonnes, although the driver usually had to walk alongside to save weight, steering by manually pushing the beast in a chosen direction! But the engines were underpowered and the tracks slipped badly on smooth sea ice. Disastrously, too, the most reliable of the motor sledges crashed through weak sea ice and sank into McMurdo Sound soon after being unloaded. Another was abandoned out on the ice shelf.

The sledge we found was later gathered up by a party of seamen from *Endeavour* and taken back to New Zealand where it is now in the Antarctic Heritage Trust Museum at Christchurch airport. I believe the remains of the petrol engine are still in the Cape Evans hut.

A VISIT BY KILLER WHALES

A pod of killer whales (orcas) took an uncomfortably close look at Derek Wright and me during a stroll we made out across the sea ice from Scott Base into McMurdo Sound one sunny January day in 1957, after *Endeavour* had been unloaded.

Penguins are a favourite snack for these mammals and they undoubtedly thought we were a particularly large and luscious variety. Whatever the reason, they turned up when we were about 1.5 kilometres out from land, walking close to the sea ice ledge that was probably less than a metre thick. At this time, in late summer, the bay ice was still breaking up and drifting out to sea.

Derek, who had been busy filming all our activities, from building Scott Base to the dog teams and tractor parties venturing out on survey trips, had wanted to take advantage of a lull to get some background film footage of Ross Island, Mount Erebus and the Royal Society Range from a distance.

I went with him to get some colour and black and white photographs, as well as to act as Derek's buddy. We had a strict rule that no one was to venture away from the base alone, in case of trouble — travelling in pairs was a must, while groups of three or four were recommended.

Just as we had decided we had shot enough film and were turning for home, the orcas arrived. They were probably attracted by the echoes of our footsteps, in the same way they apparently home in on the noise made by flocks of penguins.

Anyway, we noticed them cruising through the broken ice floes then, as they got closer, rearing up on their tails to get a better look.

Neither of us was particularly worried at first, being intent on moving around to get good shots of the whales. I was snapping away when there was a very loud curse from Derek — he had run out of film after shooting for only a few seconds! Unhappily, I soon realised I was also near the end of my last roll.

About this time, it also seemed a good idea to move back away from the ice edge as one or two of the whales began rearing out of the sea and heaving themselves on to the ice before sliding back. So we rather regretfully made our way back to shore.

Safely back at Scott Base, both Derek and I lamented to our companions about running out of film — and missing a rare opportunity to get some great close-ups of the whales. More experienced Antarctic hands assured us, however, that it may have been a lucky chance that saved us from serious trouble.

Our biologist, Ron Balham, told us quite cheerfully that this was the whales' favourite way of getting at penguins — breaking up the sea ice by either throwing themselves out of the water on to the edge of the floe or crashing up from underneath, so that the penguins fell into the sea.

Above: *The killer whales continually cruised off the edge of the ice floe, repeatedly raising themselves out of the water to take a better look.*
Left: *I took this tranquil picture of Derek Wright gazing at the Royal Society Range some 50 kilometres away, and some Adélie penguins nearby, just moments before a pod of orcas came looking for lunch. We were on the edge of the sea ice about 1.5 kilometres from land.*

Right, below and opposite: *These close-ups of the killer whales are among the few I managed to take for posterity before I unfortunately (or maybe fortunately, as it turned out) ran out of film. Otherwise, we would have stayed around to photograph them rearing up and heaving themselves in to the ice before sliding back — their way of breaking up the floes to catch dinner.*

I discovered later, when reading accounts by Scott and others, that their photographer H G Ponting had a narrow escape while trying to photograph killer whales, when members of the expedition were unloading *Terra Nova* at Cape Evans in early January 1912.

Scott had noticed half a dozen killer whales circling in the bay and called out to Ponting that he should try to get a photograph. Ponting ran toward the edge of the ice with his camera (a great big box-like affair with a heavy tripod) and as he did so the killer whales dived, then heaved up under the metre-thick ice floe, similar to the one we were standing on, breaking it into fragments, according to Scott. Ponting luckily scrambled to safety and two huskies tethered on the floe also escaped.

And three years earlier, in January 1909, during Shackleton's expedition, Raymond Priestley, the scientist who was also on Scott's last expedition, had a similar experience when camped on what they had thought was a firm ice floe near Butter Point, under the Victoria Range on the western side of McMurdo Sound. He recorded in his diary that a large school of killer whales was hopefully patrolling the water lanes, adding: 'One of them bumped directly beneath our tent, cracking the ice in all directions . . . I shall dream of killer whales for weeks.'

Quietly, Derek and I agreed that discretion could sometimes be the better part of valour and that we should take better care, next time. But, to our disappointment, orcas never came that close to either of us again.

Some of the team on the expedition branding the gentle Weddell seals.

Seals for sustenance and study

We stalked and killed Weddell seals for husky food, most of it naturally and rapidly becoming deep-frozen, ready to be stored for the winter months. There was a bonus, prized by some of us, for helping kill and cut up the seals — acquisition of the animal's penis bone! About 15 centimetres long, it was elegantly shaped like a swizzle-stick. I managed to get a set of four that, back home, I would put out with cocktails for guests and then wait for them to ask where these interestingly shaped pieces of bone had come from. Their reactions were quite amusing.

The seals we spared were branded, as cattle are, so that their migratory habits could be studied — many turned up in later years on the other side of the continent in the Weddell Sea abutting the Atlantic waters.

Jim Bates had built a portable branding furnace of fire bricks heated with a blowtorch, mounted on a small sledge that we would, as casually as possible, pull up close to a pod of seals, usually fewer than a dozen or so, that were happily minding their own business, basking on the sea ice alongside their diving holes.

Then a couple of us would grab a seal by the tail while a third expedition member, usually Ron, wielded the branding iron. A short sizzle, which we were assured the seal did not feel because of its thick blubber, and the seal would then hastily wriggle off and disappear down its diving hole to cool off. Ron used two symbols for the brand, an 'H' or an 'X' picked because they could not be confused with figures, followed by two numbers.

We always found the seals close to the sea ice, but wondered whether they could be more adventurous than they seemed. Scott recorded that in 1903 he and a survey party found a Weddell seal carcass 80 kilometres up the Ferrar Glacier from the coast at an altitude of 1500 metres. And in October 1957, the New Zealand northern sledging party discovered a perfectly preserved seal at 600 metres in the Prince Albert Mountains.

Although these seals inhabit a very large segment of the Antarctic coast they get their name, like the sea on the South American side of Antarctica, from James Weddell , a Scottish sealer who was a remarkable navigator and explorer.

Above: *A mother and her baby.*

Top: *An adult skua takes off.*
Above: *A group of young Adélie penguins at the rookery near Shackleton's hut at Cape Royds. Note the baby fluff on their heads and backs.*

Left: *Sir Hubert Wilkins in his reindeer-skin coat and pants, but wearing United States Navy thermal boots.*
Right: *Derek is wearing gear normally used by expedition members when on the trail.*

CHAPTER 9

WHAT THE WELL-DRESSED ANTARCTIC EXPLORER WORE

Sir Hubert Wilkins, a veteran early explorer who has, with some justification been called an 'enigma of polar exploration', visited McMurdo for a few days in the summer of 1957 to study the suitability of polar clothing and living conditions for the United States Army.

Then close to 70 years old, Sir Hubert cut a sartorial elegance that made the rest of us feel quite drab. He wore, as outside cold-weather gear, a three-quarter-length reindeer-skin coat that most women would have killed for. He had done so for years in both the Arctic and Antarctic.

Underneath, he wore a quilted jacket and pants and no underwear. 'It's a little rough on your hide at first,' he told me, 'but you get used to it, and it pays off when you're on the trail.'

An Australian, he had an extraordinary life of Arctic and Antarctic exploration as well as in the harsh deserts of his own country. During the First World War he proved to be a remarkably talented photographer, recording what are acknowledged to be among the best war pictures ever taken.

In April 1928, he made the longest non-stop flight ever attempted in the Arctic flying from Alaska to Spitzbergen in Norway, for which he was knighted by King George V.

In December the same year, he then made the first flight in the Antarctic, completing a series of short surveys from Graham Land on the Atlantic coast of the continent — not far from where Vivian Fuchs eventually established his trans-Antarctic base.

Sir Hubert had made his first visit to the Arctic in 1913, and had been associated with Shackleton but was probably best known for a spectacularly unsuccessful attempt to navigate a submarine called the *Nautilus* under the North Pole in 1931.

Tastes differed

Our tastes were perhaps not the same as Wilkins's, but probably no one will ever design the perfect Antarctic clothing, because needs and preferences differ widely.

Often during McMurdo Sound's salubrious summer, when the climate was more like a high alpine village, we wore just a singlet and woollen shirt, the sort of clothes one might wear skiing on a warm day in Europe, the United States or New Zealand. During the expedition all of us were continually making modifications, some of which were incorporated into the standard issue for future years.

Most of us wore, from the skin out, an open-weave string singlet that rather resembled a housewife's shopping bag and, when there was a real bite in the air, a plain woollen singlet over that. On its own, the string singlet is extremely warm and has the advantage of permitting the body to breathe freely.

Bill Hartigan, a tough Brooklyn-born news cameraman with NBC, always seemed to have a tin of anchovies in his pocket. He called them survival rations.

Perspiration is a serious issue in the Antarctic because it can freeze and chill the body. Most of us also wore, unlike Sir Hubert, long johns (underpants) that usually came in a rather revolting shade of pale red.

On top, we wore a good, thick New Zealand-wool shirt — these became popular with Americans and Australians, too — and then, perhaps, a pullover. I had a bulky, bright orange crew-neck pullover that my wife Pamela had knitted so that I wouldn't get lost in a white-out! I was extremely proud of it. That's it, in the picture of me on page 51.

On windy days when the chill factor rose sharply, or on the trail, we also wore either a light windproof anorak made of Byrd cloth — named after the United States polar pioneer Admiral Richard Byrd, which was a combination of cotton and synthetics — or a heavier down jacket that looked bulky but was surprisingly light and comfortable.

In the dry, desert-like conditions of Antarctica it was quite surprising how little clothing one needed to keep warm on a fine day, as long as there was no wind.

Derek Wright from the New Zealand Film Unit, and Bill Hartigan, the cameraman from NBS in New York, wore clothing that would also accommodate easily the various camera lenses, film, filters, light meters and so on, that burden all cameramen. On a fine day Bill preferred a type of waistcoat that also had pockets for his tins of anchovies.

Even at the South Pole, on the day we gathered to greet Fuchs and the trans-Antarctic expedition party when the weather was sunny and only about minus 25°C, I wore just a string singlet, woollen singlet and shirt, and a light anorak.

The United States naval personnel on Operation Deepfreeze wore military-designed clothing as well as cold-weather gear very similar to our own when working out on the ice. All of us favoured a double parka hood with a heavy outside fur-circlet, usually made of wolverine, which could be thrown back away from the face when the weather was fine.

Footwear and gloves presented special problems because needs varied depending upon whether you were working around the base or out on the trail.

The best all-round boot design, we found, was similar to the Eskimo mukluk, used by alpine climbers, including Ed Hillary and Tenzing for their Everest climb. It consists of a canvas outer, shod with rubber and with one or two inner layers of felt. Heavy woollen socks were usually worn.

Mukluks are only suitable in below-zero snow, however, where the snow is continually dry. Most of us wore normal heavy alpine climbing boots around the base, to cope with the inevitable snow slush, as well as on short trips around McMurdo Sound while exploring the dry valleys and glacier tongues.

The United States naval personnel had a wet-weather boot that became quite popular with those of us who could scrounge a pair when working in slushy conditions: a high double-skinned rubber boot with an air space in between that was worn without socks but was comfortably warm.

Gloves were very much a matter of preference, especially for the scientists, tractor drivers and others who had to handle instruments or mechanical components outside. Silk- or nylon-and-wool mixtures were often worn as inner gloves. Outer gloves were of leather and lined. Sir Hubert had a pair of reindeer-skin gloves with the fur on the inside.

Gloves are particularly tiresome if you are fiddling with a camera. Dr Ron Balham, the New Zealand expedition biologist and meteorologist, solved this problem by bringing down to the Antarctic half a dozen inexpensive Kodak Box Brownie cameras, which were popular at the time. The cameras had no focus or speed stops and all Ron needed to do was point the camera and knock the exposure lever with his gloved hand. When the camera's cheap

On what Ed called salubrious days, we often wore the same sort of gear one would wear at a ski resort. Here, Hillary enjoys a sunny day at McMurdo Sound.

mechanism broke in the severe cold he simply threw it away and unpacked another. Surprisingly, but undoubtedly because of the even nature of Antarctic daylight most of the time, he got some splendid photographs.

But there was one essential feature: all our outer gloves had a furry patch on the back to rub away the eternal icicle that gathers on the tip of every polar explorer's nose, no matter how good the parka.

Snappy dresser

I gained a splendid cold-weather jacket through an odd incident that occurred about three months before the New Zealand expedition was due to sail south.

I was idling away in the *Herald* reporters' room in Auckland one quiet Sunday afternoon when I was assigned by the news editor to interview an American clothing manufacturer from New York, who was passing through on his way to the Olympic Games being held in Melbourne later in the year. The New Yorker was spending the day with the owner of a large department store (who was also a large advertiser) and it seemed diplomatic to the news editor for me to scratch out a brief story about the visit. As I said, it was a quiet Sunday, with not much news around.

I cannot forget the name of the clothing brand — McGregor Sportswear — although it has, as far as I know, long disappeared from store shelves. At that time it was breaking new ground, attempting to entice young men to dress a little more adventurously and break away from the drab colours we normally wore in those days. The manufacturer was, I believe, a member of the United States Olympic Committee.

I rather fancied that I was already a snappy dresser. On that wintry Sunday, I was wearing my customary style of casual clothes which consisted, on this occasion, of a black woollen shirt with a thin white check, and a bright yellow tie, accompanied by the standard grey flannel pants and a moss-green tweed sports jacket. Oh yes, and light brown suede shoes. I kid you not!

So you will not be surprised that when I walked into the New Yorker's hotel room, he took one look at me and said frankly: 'Son, you're a mess!'

With that promising beginning the interview went rather well, and later that evening I filed what I thought was a quirky, humorous piece on what this New Yorker thought of New Zealand men's fashion and how he was going to change it.

During the course of the interview, the local department-store owner had mentioned that I had been chosen to join Ed Hillary's Antarctic expedition and, apparently delighted by the interview, our New Yorker insisted on having his local representatives make me a jacket suitable for the hip Antarctic explorer.

What they eventually ran up was a very comfortable, warm jacket useful around Scott Base and, later, the Ruapehu Ski Club in New Zealand, of which I was a member. Eventually, one of my daughters borrowed it and I haven't seen it since.

I'm wearing the jacket made by my American clothing manufacturer.

'In Memoriam', reads the cross that was erected on Observation Hill by the survivors of Scott's fatal expedition in 1912. From this hill overlooking Hut Point, they watched in vain for signs of Scott and his party returning from the South Pole.

CHAPTER 10

REMINDERS OF EARLIER EXPLORERS

Antarctica is not only dotted with the remains of historic huts but also permanent memorials to early explorers: some are legends, others are team members little known except by their families and historians. Several are scattered around McMurdo Sound, quite close to Scott Base.

The best known, and one of the most accessible of all the memorials, is the three-metre-high wooden cross made from jarrah erected to Robert Falcon Scott and his four companions on Observation Hill, not far from Discovery Hut at Hut Point in McMurdo Sound.

The cross stands on the 225-metre summit — it's quite a steep little climb between the United States and New Zealand bases — from where members of Scott's expedition took turns to look fruitlessly south across the Ross Ice Shelf during February and March 1912, hoping to see their companions returning.

Underneath the names of Scott, Wilson, Oates, Bowers and Evans it bears the legend from Tennyson's *Ulysses*: 'To strive, to seek, to find but not to yield', which could be the enduring memorial for all who ventured south in those earlier days.

Not far away, on Danger Slope near Hut Point, is Vince's Cross that marks the spot where George Vince, a British seaman with Scott's first expedition, lost his footing and slid over the cliff into the icy bay. His body was never recovered. Derek Wright and I could both testify that the slope is dangerously slippery when a windy day makes the ground icy. I slipped while taking a photograph of the cross, he grabbed me and then fell over as well and it was only some frantic scrabbling that halted us uncomfortably near the cliff edge.

Also close by is a cross erected by members of Operation Deepfreeze in 1955 that has come to represent the American men who have died in various nearby accidents. And there's a cross at Wind Vane Hill on Cape Evans, erected in memory of three members of the Ross Sea Party that was intended to back up Shackleton's ill-fated 1914–16 trans-Antarctic attempt.

There are also several sacred sites in the Ross Sea–McMurdo Sound area, the earliest being where Borchgrevink's shore party landed in February 1899, at Ridley Beach on Cape Adare on the north-western coast. They were forced to land there because of heavy sea ice, but they could scarcely have chosen a more inhospitable place, hemmed in by steep cliffs and said to be one of the windiest on the continent.

Their huts still stand there, in spite of the atrocious weather, as does a simple iron cross and brass plaque marking the first grave in the whole of Antarctica, that of their biologist, Nicolai Hanson, who died of pneumonia during the winter of 1899.

Much further east, past Cape Royds, in Terra Nova Bay is Inexpressible Island where there is a rock shelter built by members of Scott's 1910–13 expedition on a survey trip, as well as a nearby cave where they spent the winter of 1912. Still further east, and inland at Mount Betty in the Queen Maud Range, is Amundsen's Cairn, built by Amundsen and his companions on 6 January 1912, during their return from the South Pole, which they were the first to reach the previous 16 December.

Right: *This memorial at Hut Point commemorates the servicemen from Operation Deepfreeze who have died in the region since 1955.*
Far right: *Vince's Cross marks the spot where British seaman George Vince slipped to his death during Scott's expedition in 1902. A husky died with him.*

Historic hut found by Hillary's 'Old Firm'

In March 1957, after the route up to the Polar Plateau had been proven and *Endeavour* had sailed home with the summer party, Ed Hillary — accompanied by Peter Mulgrew, Murray Ellis and Jim Bates — found on a tractor-testing expedition to Cape Crozier on the eastern tip of Ross Island, the remains of the stone hut built during the winter of 1911 by Edward Wilson, Birdie Bowers and Apsley Cherry-Garrard.

These remains were also a permanent memorial to the old concept of heroic exploration, in the view of expedition members.

All the New Zealand summer support party, including myself, had just returned to New Zealand and Ed had decided to test, before winter set in, just how well our trusty Ferguson tractors would stand up to a long trip in rough, testing conditions by travelling to Cape Crozier where there is a large emperor penguin colony.

Emperor penguins are quite extraordinary. Unlike other species of penguin they spend most of their life at sea, feeding not only on krill, which is the staple food of whales, but also fish and crustaceans. They have established rookeries where they congregate in March to breed but they do not nest in the accepted sense, instead congregating on the sea ice nearby. A single egg is laid in May, carried on the top of the father's feet and kept warm by a bare patch of skin on the father's breast.

Going to Crozier was a bold move on Ed's part. Wilson's party had travelled from Cape Evans to Crozier to study the emperor penguins during the depths of winter and, during the six-week, 225-kilometre journey, had suffered almost unbelievable hardships from constant gale-force winds, blizzards and temperatures as low as minus 25°C. Their experiences are graphically recalled in Cherry-Garrard's book *The Worst Journey in the World.*

When the New Zealanders reached the cape they searched in vain for the hut in high winds and low temperatures over an area of five square kilometres, eventually finding the 60-centimetre-high stone walls and remains of the tattered green canvas roof just 150 metres from their own camp.

Inside was a three-metre-long sledge with all the leather straps and lashings perfectly preserved, some emperor penguin carcasses (probably the remains of a few dinners), and dozens of small items including a pick-axe, a vacuum flask that Ed said was as good as new, clinical and meteorological thermometers and three rolls of unexposed film marked to be developed before May 1911. All are now preserved in the Antarctic Heritage Trust Museum in Christchurch, New Zealand.

Six months later, in September and with winter over, Harry Ayres, Murray Douglas and Ron Balham took two dog teams from Scott Base over to Cape Crozier to revisit the emperor penguin colony but again they ran into filthy weather and were forced to lie up, at one stage taking 10 days to travel 80 kilometres. Balham reported that the colony had grown from 200 penguins, when Wilson's party visited, to more than 1000, not counting newly hatched chicks. And, just as Cherry-Garrard had done, he brought back three unhatched emperor eggs.

Also during September, Hillary, Mulgrew, Bates and Ellis again set out to test the tractors, this time travelling west to the foot of the Ferrar Glacier, Ed Hillary's early choice for Scott Base but abandoned because of difficult access. All were to make up the South Pole tractor party that later in the year Ed dubbed The Old Firm.

Relaxing on a Saturday night at Scott Base. Jim Bates (centre), our hardworking and often ingenious diesel mechanic and spare time inventor, Bernie Gunn (right), one of our geologists, and the author before his moustache was removed following a warning from Peter Mulgrew. That is a photograph of Robert Falcon Scott on the shelf behind us.

STRANGE DRINKING HABITS AND GOURMET MEALS

Travelling south on a United States ice-breaker during my third trip to the Antarctic in December 1957, I carried on board an anonymous case containing 11 bottles of Gordon's gin and one bottle of dry vermouth — I rather fancied very dry martinis in those days. The case needed to be inconspicuous because United States naval ships are 'dry', whether at sea or in port.

I'd been briefly summonsed back to civilisation by my newspaper during what they considered a no-news period after the New Zealand tractor team had left Scott Base and was slowly picking its way up the Skelton Glacier to the Polar Plateau.

The recall was because New Zealand was in the middle of a general election and my real job at the time included writing political analysis. So I flew back for a couple of weeks and then managed to hitch a ride south again on the ice-breaker. The Race to the Pole controversy had not yet broken, of course.

As a journalist attached to the United States Navy I had been given the courtesy rank of lieutenant-commander, which was really only an administrative device to define what berthing or transportation priority I was entitled to — in this case, one of two sleeping cabins in a small suite that shared a slightly larger day cabin.

My companion was a genial priest from the notorious south side of Chicago who confided in me that his archbishop had assigned him to Antarctic duty as penance for accepting a large, white Cadillac from his parishioners as a thank-you for some unspecified services he had performed.

It was a couple of weeks before Christmas, this was a dry ice-breaker and as we unpacked we eyed each other cautiously until I confessed to my case of martini, whereupon the priest winked and opened a case of communion wine, which turned out to be packed with jars of rye whisky. I think it's safe to disclose now that during the voyage to McMurdo we were visited by virtually all the ship's officers, except the captain and his executive officer.

From several brief sojourns on other United States naval ships, both in the Antarctic and, later, off Vietnam, I learned at the cost of several splitting hangovers that firewater can be brewed almost anywhere from anything, especially in chief warrant-officers' quarters.

Almost always, though, navy coffee left a great deal to be desired, having a strong relationship with the weak, insipid stuff they still serve back in the United States. The most pleasant officers' mess I ever experienced, much later on, was on a ship that had recently completed a tour of duty off Japan, where all the officers had become enthusiastic tea drinkers.

Alcohol was of no interest to our expedition's field teams in the Antarctic, except perhaps for some medicinal spirits in their supplies, and was generally not of much importance to the rest of the expedition members, either. Drinking indiscriminately was, naturally, out of the question.

Beer, however, was a genuine thirst quencher in the dry, desert-like conditions of McMurdo Sound and we had carried down a large store in *Endeavour*. This was stacked in the covered tunnels connecting the huts, along with much of the winter's food supplies, where the atmosphere constantly resembled a chilly refrigerator. Consequently the water component in the beer froze into a large lump and bottles had to be brought into the warm living quarters to thaw before we could drink them.

Booze in any form was viewed rather differently by Operation Deepfreeze military personnel, for whom the Antarctic assignment was often regarded as just another, if rather more arduous, chore of service. Drinking was allowed at Antarctic bases, but only under strict supervision, and usually only to celebrate a national holiday. Consequently, most had a keen interest in tracking down any likely source.

Supervised drinking was, at least in those days, confined to rather watery brews of beer. On 'rest and recreation' days, United States naval ships cruising in Antarctic waters often 'parked' for a brief period at the edge of some convenient ice shelf or glacier tongue. Crew would then stand around on the ice drinking beer, cooking up hot dogs and hamburgers and generally observing the illusion that they were ashore in a port.

Invitations to visit *Endeavour* while she was berthed in McMurdo Sound were keenly sought, because the Royal New Zealand Navy officers' ward room was definitely not dry and was sometimes, quite definitely, afloat. Crew were treated rather less leniently, being issued with limited rations of beer but nevertheless we were able to entertain enlisted Americans occasionally.

In McMurdo I met a senior Surgeon Captain of the United States Navy, a man of Russian parentage whose rather strange task, considering his qualifications — apart from being able to produce a remarkable martini from whatever ingredients he found available — was to make a report on the historic huts around McMurdo and to collect some Adélie and emperor penguins for American zoos.

I've unfortunately forgotten the finer points of his martini mixes, but I remember him once producing a beaker of medicinal ethyl alcohol, unwrapping two rolls of Lifesavers and saying, 'now, first you throw away all but the red ones . . .' A jar of olives was also essential.

Little luxuries

Good food becomes of increasing importance for people isolated from most of the other pleasant things of life, and it was no different in McMurdo Sound. At Scott Base, the best New Zealand lamb, beef, bacon and other cuts were stored away, well refrigerated, for the long, dark winter months. There was also a quantity of meat treated in what the Meat Producers Board called 'a new dehydration process' to last the eight months before fresh food could be shipped in again from New Zealand.

No fewer than 600 dozen eggs were chilled, along with scores of cases of tinned fruit and vegetables — there were no frozen foods in those days, such as we now find in every supermarket. And New Zealand beekeepers — no doubt because Ed was one of them — had donated a staggering quarter of a tonne of honey.

There were lots of little luxury items, too, all of which helped the creative efforts of Buck, our cook, and the budding gourmet chefs who competed regularly at producing the most exotic Sunday dinner. Limited quantities of wine and brandy were usually drunk at these dinners, at which aspiring after-dinner speakers tried out their skills.

Interestingly, we all found that we developed a sweet tooth, often preferring cocoa drinks, or a special blend of lemonade that had been brewed with lots of sugar, to coffee. Tea, in spite of being made with powdered milk, was always popular.

Eating American

Living conditions were similar, but the food was very different at the United States naval base in McMurdo Sound. All the resources the navy could provide meant there was a much greater variety of food served up in the Williams' mess hall than at Scott Base.

Tuna seemed to be a staple, whether poached or grilled. Chickens, turkeys, hams, spare ribs, steaks were plentiful, and for special occasions pigs' knuckles were a favourite of George Dufek. I recall, too, meat and fruit pies and a whole range of goodies from a large on-site bakery.

There was no ice-cream at Scott Base, but ice-cream as a dessert was standard fare at Williams where they had a specially installed maker that worked constantly to produce sundaes served up with all sorts of tinned fruits, chocolate and whipped (from powder) cream. No wonder an invitation to visit Williams was so prized.

Personally, after longish spells with the United States Navy I never wanted to see tuna or southern fried chicken again — or have chocolate cake served up for breakfast. I did, however, fall completely for something quite new to me: marmalade spread on crispy bacon with hot dogs and eggs, sunny-side up.

Right: *The crew of* Endeavour *enjoy some rest and relaxation, joined by some expedition members, along with Captain Kirkwood (in the duffel coat far left) and Ed Hillary (facing forward far right).*

Antarctica's inhabitants make good eating

We discovered that, although Antarctica has few native inhabitants, what there are make good eating. This may shock readers, but 50 years ago it was regarded as quite correct to live off the land or, rather, the snow and ice.

At Scott Base seal steak was regarded as a delicacy and the northern survey trail party were delighted when they came upon a large seal rookery during their trip because it meant a welcome break for both them and their huskies from pemmican — a concentrated food of dried meat, berries and pulverised rendered fat — and biscuits.

A kindly description of pemmican, invented by American Indians, is that it tastes like wet putty,

but it is packed with vitamins and no one has yet starved by eating it. New Zealand nutritionists dug up and manufactured an old formula originated, it was claimed, by Admiral Byrd that tasted okay and certainly both men and dogs remained healthy.

Buck Bucknell, our Scott Base cook, had been given a number of recipes by Raoul Desprez, who had been a cook at the French base in Adélie Land, and he served most of them up during the long winter months, including seal.

There is no fishy taste to seal meat but it needs to be drained well and the fat removed. The liver, especially from a milk seal, was prized and brains were pan-fried in browned butter and covered

with a meunier sauce or put in a puff-pastry pie with béchamel, grated cheese and breadcrumbs.

I never experienced eating Adélie or emperor penguins. In fact, I'm sure I would not have done so except in a dire emergency, but I was told that their liver was as delicate as calf liver and the breasts were cut into steaks and cooked as small fillets. 'Never,' warned M. Desprez, 'roast penguin meat.'

Skuas, the aggressive camp cleaners who are the only native birds in Antarctica, also made good eating, especially if the small steaks from their breasts were marinated in wine.

Camped out on the Polar Plateau. Expedition members stayed within the warmth of tents when resting, but huskies seemed to enjoy the cold.

CHAPTER

12

PREPARING FOR THE GREAT ADVENTURE

Late January 1957, and autumn was now moving in at Scott Base, heralded by magnificent sunsets gradually extending from just a few minutes as the sun dipped below the southern horizon to several hours as the days grew shorter. Very soon all the summer construction and support parties would depart.

But there were still a lot of finishing touches to complete, as well as some sightseeing. Everybody — the construction team, scientists and general hands — had been working long hours and some now went off climbing and exploring around Ross Island, or gave a hand loading aircraft in the hope of a sightseeing flight.

Ed was, as usual, everywhere. The three dog teams, supported by the air force crew, John, Bill, Wally and Peter, were racing against the coming late-autumn storms, flying constantly to support the field parties who were probing through the mountains to find a safe route to the Polar Plateau, and establishing and stocking the depots.

Brooke, Ellis, Ayres and Douglas, with 18 huskies, were slogging up the Skelton Glacier, quite literally going where no man had ever gone before, with the intention of gaining the Polar Plateau and establishing a depot there — later to be known as Depot 270. Meanwhile Miller and Carlyon, with another dog team, were proving the route across the Ross Ice Shelf to Skelton Depot at the foot of the glacier, some 290 kilometres from our base.

In addition, Bernie Gunn and Guy Warren, the expedition's two geologists, and Arnold Heine, a member of the summer party who was also an experienced mountaineer, had been flown to the Skelton to examine the massive exposed rock faces of some of the mountains in the region. Because most of the Antarctic is a desert with, for example, only a a few centimetres of precipitation a year recorded around McMurdo, the snow is very dry and unable to stick to steep slopes, exposing some amazing coloured mountain faces.

During this month-long field trip the trio also made the first ascent of a major peak on the Antarctic continent, Mount Harmsworth, just over 2700 metres in the Worcester Range. Mount Erebus on Ross Island had been climbed twice, by parties from Scott's and Shackleton's expeditions, and was soon to be climbed again by New Zealanders. Harmsworth had been named after Alfred Harmsworth, later Lord Northcliffe, whose newspaper empire co-sponsored Scott's last expedition.

On 9 February, one day before the Harmsworth climb and some 145 kilometres further south-west, the two advance dog teams had finally reached the Polar Plateau, 2400 metres up at the top of the Skelton, where they reported a vast, featureless snow plain with the temperature hovering around minus 15–20°C.

Ed lost no time. That day he and Arthur flew up in the Beaver piloted by John and, after having some difficulty tracking the field party in spite of both radar and radio contact, eventually made the first landing on the Plateau. They were supported by Bill and Wally in the little Auster, which flew shotgun.

While the Auster circled overhead, John made a textbook landing beside the tents with the four men waving mightily. The wind was gathering force and no one wanted to stand around for very long, although Arthur, true to form, handed over some mail he had carried up, while Ed outlined his plans to stock the depot as quickly as possible.

The Beaver had no trouble taking off and Bill then landed the Auster easily enough beside the camp, but it was a different story when he took off after a few minutes. The Auster was operating at just about the limit of its range and, Ed told us later, took a frighteningly long run before it finally staggered into the air. On the spot, it was decided that only the Beaver would operate over the Plateau.

Stocking eight tonnes of fuel and food at Depot 270 began almost immediately and was kept up around the clock.

Three days after the initial landing on the Plateau, Depot 270 was completed and marked both visually and with a beacon so that it could be easily found early next spring. Then it would be completely stocked, ready to supply both Ed's trek to the Pole and, later, Fuchs's crossing party.

On 13 February, with relief, Richard, Harry, the two Murrays and their huskies made no delay in leaving Depot 270 and descending down through The Portal, as the broad head of the glacier became known, to the relatively warmer climate of the Skelton Neve where they were to continue with their mapping of the glacier.

Later as they slowly descended toward the Skelton

Depot they were joined by Bernie, Guy and Arnold, and eventually by Bob and Roy who had mapped a safe route across the Ross Ice Shelf. During the next week Arnold was flown out because he had to catch *Endeavour* before it departed. Peter Mulgrew flew in for a few days to test the field radios, which were gradually proving more efficient, replacing Murray Ellis, and then he returned to Scott Base on a supply flight.

By now, late February, the weather was definitely packing up with continual, although localised, snow storms making surveying work and visits by the aircraft difficult. On 28 February, all the parties were recalled and the Beaver flew in to pick up Harry plus his team of huskies and his tent. It returned some hours later for Bob, another husky team and a load of gear. One last trip was needed to pick up Roy, Murray, Richard and the remaining 11 huskies. A tent full of unneeded gear was left at the depot.

Endeavour had sailed on 24 February with most of the summer crew, following a farewell party on 20 February which became a very exuberant affair. I arranged to stay on with Derek and a couple of others for almost two more weeks, writing wrap-up pieces, and eventually we returned to Christchurch in early March on one of the last Globemaster flights for the season.

By then the ice in McMurdo Sound had broken up in autumn storms, almost back to the airstrip near the Ross Ice Shelf. It would soon disappear, and would not be rebuilt until McMurdo Sound had frozen over again, in seven months' time.

Back at Scott Base, Ed was getting everything bedded down for the winter, which included a number of field activities for both dogs and tractors within a range of about 80 kilometres. To give the Ferguson tractors a thorough try-out, Ed and a small team took a trip to Cape Crozier on the eastern tip of Ross Island, where the ice shelf met the Ross Sea, which I've recounted in Chapter 10.

Life away from the base

Confined to Scott Base by a blizzard one day in October 1957, I became a shade introspective because even though we were blessed with better communications, life away from our bases was still grim. It remains so today. It was often a struggle just to exist in conditions that were little different from what they had been 50 years previously. The following is what I wrote:

Sudden and bitter contrasts dominate life in the Antarctic. In the huts living is pleasant, almost civilised; outside awaits a knife-edged wind and a treacherous terrain. And the two are never reconciled.

On a fine day McMurdo Sound is breathtakingly beautiful. Forty miles to the westward the Royal Society Range is a rocky wall, 10,000 to 13,000 feet high [3810 m] and full of delicate colour that puts the magnificent Southern Alps in New Zealand to shame. Mt Erebus, the 12,500 foot active volcano to the north, is a huge ice-cream cone and, to the south, is a hint of the flat featureless ice shelf cut across by White Island and Mount Discovery.

In a blizzard it can be hell; snow-filled air plucks at parkas and the wind numbs the face and hands to the point where no feeling remains.

Back home, water is something that comes from a tap. It will never be that again to men who have wintered here. In the Antarctic water is one of the rarest of luxuries to be hoarded and used miserly.

To get water means going out to the ice shelf and carting in snow by tractor, then half an hour's work shovelling it into melters. On a fine day it can be a reasonably pleasant chore; when the temperature is around 30 below and there is a 20-knot wind blowing it is deadening, killing labour. Washing has to be cut to a minimum and even cleaning teeth becomes a manoeuvre.

In the huts are warmth, music, books, plenty of absorbing work and good company — friendships [and, as I found later, enemies] *are being made down here that will last throughout life. A woollen shirt is sufficient in the 65°F, [18°C] thermostatically controlled atmosphere. It could be a camp anywhere in the world — with this difference: there is no leave, no going into town to get away from it all for a few hours.*

Putting on and taking off clothing takes up a sizeable amount of each day, if one's tasks lie outside. It is time-wasting but essential. Anyone who decides a two or three minute dash outside is not worth three or four minutes of struggling into and out of a parka is risking frostbitten ears and fingers and the certainty of being chilled to the bone.

Every day the huskies have to be fed. That means cutting up stiff, board-hard seal meat with a cross-cut saw or an axe and enduring the wind and the cold for an hour or more.

Scientific instruments have to be checked, no matter what the weather. Now and then someone has to climb the anemometer mast in a cutting wind, feet and hands fumbling on the icy pegs, to repair the recorder. And there is the long, dreary aurora watch when eyelids droop as no enticing coloured lights dance across the sky.

Flight Sergeant Wally Tarr worked all winter in a heated packing case he fixed up for himself down by the airstrip. He checked instruments and made new parts for the Auster and Beaver aircraft. Between the camp and his packing case was a quarter of a mile [400 m] of snow and ice, a steep 60-foot [18 m] slope that seemed to increase considerably when a stiff wind was blowing across it, and a couple of tidal cracks in the sea ice that began to look like baby crevasses in bad weather. Once, after a blizzard, Wally found his packing case buried 15 feet [4.5 m] under snow drifts. It took days of patient work with a tractor to dig it out and winch it up to the new surface.

But there were the Sunday night dinners — when our cook, Selwyn [Buck] Bucknell, had a night off and expedition members took turns to prepare the meal — that came to be regarded as contributing to the best night

of the week. Toasts were made and drunk, after-dinner speakers blossomed. And there was the weekly radio news programme — beamed directly down from New Zealand with someone's wife and children on hand to chat as best they could about life back home.

But, over it all for the trail parties, there was the need to prepare for the summer journeys of exploration.

I took this aerial photograph looking directly south from about 1525 metres in late October 1957, when McMurdo Sound was still largely frozen over. Cape Armitage, Hut Point and Observation Hill are the furthest ice-free promontories in the centre of the picture and beyond are Black and White islands. Mount Erebus rises from the left and in the top right of the picture is Minna Bluff, leading down from the Royal Society Range, and Mount Discovery. Cape Royds and Shackleton's Nimrod Hut are out of the picture, bottom left, while Cape Evans, with Scott's Hut, is in the foreground, free of ice.

Flying home was not uneventful

The flight home turned out to be an adventure in itself. The Globemaster, one of the huge air freighters that had worked hard all summer flying people, supplies and equipment from America via New Zealand, and then airdropping supplies to the South Pole, creaked and groaned as we climbed to around 2500 metres over the Southern Ocean for the 13-hour flight home. It had been through a tough few months, tested under extreme conditions.

The handful of passengers in the vast cargo hold settled down as best we could on makeshift web seats and wrapped ourselves in blankets. The Globemaster clearly was not pressurised, nor did it have the luxury of heating, and most of us drifted off to an uneasy sleep.

About five hours out, I was wakened by my old friend Derek Wright who silently pulled me to a window and pointed. One starboard, propeller-driven engine had been closed down and the other, shedding oil, looked as if it wasn't turning very effectively.

'We're going back to McMurdo,' Derek shouted in my ear over the noise. 'We've dropped to about 3500 feet [1000 m]. Going to take another five or six hours, they reckon.' Most of the other passengers were still asleep but two American crewmen were in the front of the hold, calmly assembling survival gear. Survival was a notoriously ambiguous word among aircrew — we all knew that the seas below were deadly.

Anyway, not to make too much out of an incident that had occurred several times before to other crews, we eventually limped back to McMurdo, exhausted, and fell asleep in one of the now empty huts at the American base that were used during the summer. About 10 hours later we were on our way again, trying to appear hearty and cracking jokes but, I assure you, with our fingers firmly crossed. The Globemasters were clearly as exhausted as we were.

Anyway, the next flight to Christchurch International Airport was uneventful, if long and dreary. We arrived in the early morning and I soon discovered that a regular flight to Auckland was leaving within half an hour. There were no security or customs checks in those days and after telephoning home to announce my unexpected arrival, and without attempting to change out of my quite dirty anorak, woollen shirt, heavy drill pants and alpine boots, I clambered aboard with my kit bag.

I'm sure I was quite malodorous, but the businessman I sat next to politely pretended not to notice and seemed much more interested in questioning me about life at Scott Base, so the next two hours passed quite pleasantly.

It would be almost exactly seven months before I returned with Admiral Dufek in his personal Skymaster DC4, on one of the first flights back to McMurdo for the following summer season.

Meanwhile, the 23 men at Scott Base, along with the larger Deepfreeze contingent at Williams, were settling in for their long winter of preparation for the great adventures ahead.

Left: *As summer advanced and the sea ice broke up, the airstrip built in McMurdo Sound became endangered and then disappeared. This is early summer, looking toward the American and New Zealand bases at Hut Point.*
Below: *By late summer the airstrip had all but vanished.*
Opposite: *A United States Globemaster.*

Flight to Depot 270 on the Polar Plateau

Two days after those first flights to the Polar Plateau Depot, I accompanied Bill Cranfield on a supply trip when the weather was extremely unpleasant. A brisk wind was blowing, heightening the chill factor.

Bill and I took off from Scott Field (as we called the airstrip) about 3 a.m. with three 44-gallon drums of fuel and some boxes of pemmican for the huskies for the 320-kilometre flight, heading south toward Mount Discovery, then eastward to the Koetlitz Glacier that ran to the top of the Skelton Glacier. The following is the account from my diary:

It's a bleak place. To our right were the jumbled mountains of the Royal Society Range running away to the coast but to our left there was only one outcrop that marks the top of the Skelton and then just a featureless white surface stretching about 1000 miles [1600 km] to the South Pole. It is beautiful up there, in spite of the bleakness — the colours are pastel and in limited shades but they have an unearthly feeling. The weather was packing up with a strengthening wind whipping up the snow.

We were flying at 8700 feet [2650 m], just 700 feet [200 m] above the surface, and searching for the tiny camp, just three tents and some dogs tethered in the snow, was difficult. Finally I saw them — or rather, the shadow of the tents over to the right and then one husky that had got loose and was running across the marked-out landing strip.

As we made our approach the weather closed in and it was just about impossible to see the surface because of the snow drifting up about 20 feet [6 m]. Bill made a second pass, there was a sudden bump and we were down — and then the fun started. He opened the throttle to taxi to the camp and the Beaver stuck solidly to the surface. We looked at each other and Bill said: 'Well, it'll be a long walk back to base.'

Inside the Beaver the temperature was minus 10°F

[minus 23°C]. We put on our extra gloves, drew up our parkas and climbed outside — minus 32°F, or 64° of frost [minus 35°C] and a bitter wind of about 20 knots. I was well dressed up: string singlet with a woollen one on top, my 'gay nineties' drawers, battledress pants with windproof pants over them, a woollen shirt, pullover, down under-jacket and parka. Bill was similarly dressed.

We didn't waste much time. First Bill produced a roll of strong cord and we pulled this under each of the aircraft's skis — one on each side — to free them from the snow. What happens is that the friction of the skis melts the snow, which then freezes again once the aircraft stops, tending to stick it to the surface.

Then, as Bill and I threw out the first drum two figures, well padded up, appeared from one of the tents, Murray Douglas and Richard Brooke. You don't go outside more than you have to at those temperatures.

Actually it was quite bearable, even with the wind, but my face was cold. Richard and Murray were wearing face masks. Within minutes ice gathered thickly over my eyebrows, lashes and moustache, caused by breath condensation, and there was ice covering the fur lining of my parka. Anyway, we unloaded and had a quick word with Peter Mulgrew, who was in his sleeping bag in his tent talking to Scott Base on the radio.

The snow was quite soft underfoot with each step sinking in four or five inches [about 11 cm]. After we had unloaded the drums of fuel I scooped up a handful of powdery snow and tried to make a snowball, but it was so dry it just spilled through my gloved fingers. Because I was not wearing a face mask my breath at that temperature caught sharply at the back of my throat, while I could feel ice on my lips. We were back into the aircraft after perhaps 20 minutes.

The Beaver took a while to start, with Bill doing all sorts of usual and unusual things to the throttle, propeller pitch and so on but she's a grand little aircraft and with the engine thoroughly warmed she soon began to move — hellishly slowly, but she did move.

By this time the wind had freshened considerably, visibility was absolutely zero and Bill had to make an instrument takeoff right into the teeth of the snowstorm. At 8000 feet [2500 m] it wasn't the most enjoyable experience but Bill did a first-class job, although he later admitted it was mostly by feel because, with the cold, the instruments were reacting as slowly as the aircraft.

Twenty feet [6 m] up and we were in the clear, in brilliant sunshine, so Bill agreed to my pleas and we deviated over to the Ferrar Glacier and descended toward Butter Point. Hell, we would never have got up it with either the dogs or tractors; the surface is blue ice with crevasses and some formidable ice cliffs.

But the scenery is just breathtaking. Huge mountains, up to 13,000 feet [4000 m] towering above us and coloured in fantastic shades from light yellow to rich reds and browns. Some of the exposed faces are divided into strata so a mountain's side becomes striped like a marzipan biscuit.

From Butter Point we flew along the edge of the glacier where icebergs were breaking off, then had a good look at the Dailey Islands and watched killer whales playing in the sound. There were seven emperor penguins standing on an ice floe looking, perhaps thoughtfully, at our strange presence. Then on home for a much delayed breakfast.

Fuchs's Royal Air Force Otter on the New Zealand ice strip not far from Scott Base toward the end of the expedition. Because the base was overcrowded, a couple of the crew chose to sleep in tents nearby. In the far distance is Mount Discovery, 2770 metres, at the base of Minna Bluff, with Black Island, 1110 metres, and White Island, 700 metres, in front.

Ron Balham drove one of the Ferguson tractors as far as the Skelton Glacier Depot, standing in for Jim Bates who had to remain temporarily at Scott Base until his replacement engineer arrived from New Zealand to look after summer maintenance.

CHAPTER 13

AWAY AT LAST

Ed Hillary and his seasoned tractor companions Murray Ellis and Peter Mulgrew finally left Scott Base for the Polar Plateau in the late afternoon of Monday 14 October 1957, but without Jim Bates, the fourth member of the Old Firm.

Ed had planned to leave a few days earlier with Jim, the expedition's hard-working and sometimes brilliantly innovative mechanic, but delayed departure in the hope that Jim's summer replacement at the base would arrive from New Zealand on one of the first American aircraft to fly in, the previous week.

But there was a big demand for the first aircraft seats and when the replacement failed to turn up, Ron Balham, biologist and meteorologist, who was also well experienced with dogs and tractors, agreed to take Jim's place as far as the Polar Plateau, Depot 270. Ron was an old friend of mine: his father, of Belgian descent, whom we schoolboys called Froggy Balham, had taught us French at Wellington College.

The day was bleak and very grey but calm, as we gathered around the vehicles that would attempt to blaze a trail for Vivian Fuchs's party: three Ferguson tractors, a Weasel, the caboose and seven sledges laden with fuel, food, tents and survival gear.

The caboose had been built largely by Ed and Peter to sleep four, or five at a pinch. It was a metal frame on skis, about four metres by 1.5 metres covered with plywood and then British racing-green canvas.

'It means we should be able to live quite well,' Ed said as he rather proudly showed me the interior. Normally, though, except for Ed and occasionally Peter, most of the party pitched tents to sleep, using the caboose only when the occasional blizzard sprang up unexpectedly, or to snatch some rest on the trail while others drove.

It had adequate cooking facilities using a primus and, for the time, quite sophisticated and powerful radio equipment Peter had developed to keep in touch with Scott Base and the other field parties. It had also been well insulated after Ed found, on an earlier test run, that the temperature inside was only slightly higher than it was outside. But soon, after they reached the Skelton, they found the ventilation left something to be desired when they all suffered mild headaches from carbon monoxide poisoning caused by the primus. A larger roof vent fixed that.

True to Ed's theory that it was safer to travel during the night hours — the sun was now up for about 20 hours a day, with breathtaking sunsets and sunrises filling in the remaining hours on fine days — the tractor train left Scott Base late afternoon, farewelled by quite a sizeable crowd of Americans as well as the entire Scott Base contingent. Bob Miller and George Marsh, who were to be flown in to the Skelton Depot later in the week, had harnessed up their dog teams and they ran alongside the tractors for a kilometre

Just before the New Zealanders' departure from Scott Base, the NBC America cameraman persuaded Admiral Dufek to interview Ed Hillary.

or two in order to give them some exercise.

The Old Firm were initially following the route that Scott and his ill-fated party travelled 46 years earlier, as I reminded my readers, but after Minna Bluff, would turn westward toward the Skelton over the trail blazed by New Zealand dog teams the previous summer.

This was the first time the Fergusons had ventured far over the Ross Ice Shelf, but they had been well tested on the very tough autumn run to Cape Crozier earlier in the year. In addition, in September, before the influx of all the summer visitors, Ed had taken them with five men across McMurdo Sound to Butter Point and then up the Royal Society Range coast to Gneiss Point, adding a couple of tonnes, in all, of food and kerosene to depots there, which would be used by the northern husky field teams doing geological work later in the summer.

After the group left Scott Base, the grey weather soon went away and the tractor train made good and steady progress, bowling along quite encouragingly over the hard-packed ice which, the tractor drivers had discovered, suited the Fergusons much better than softer snow, even though the ride was bumpy and often uncomfortable. Unfortunately, they later hit soft snow when the tractors showed an aggravating tendency to become bogged and had to tow each other free.

A New Zealand cabinet minister, Jim McAlpine, had arrived in McMurdo on a fact-finding trip (he was Minister for Aviation) as the guest of Admiral George Dufek and consequently, only three days after Ed's departure, George decided to fly McAlpine out to see how things were progressing, inviting me along for the ride.

It was a lovely sunny day and we caught up with the team off Minna Bluff after less than ten minutes' flying, circling around a few times and then making an easy landing. The minister jumped out to offer his best wishes for the trip and to take advantage of a

photo opportunity while I had a quick yarn with Ron and Ed, who courteously handled all the formalities but was visibly anxious to get a move on. It was all rather much ado about nothing much, yet!

Within five days Ed's party reached the Skelton Depot, but not before repeated mechanical problems

with the Weasel caused annoying delays. Bob and George were waiting with the dog teams, and also Jim Bates, who had been flown in the previous day. The weather was typical of early spring, fluctuating between lovely ski-resort weather slightly above freezing, and then switching abruptly to murky conditions well below freezing.

Now the Fergusons were to be tested on the Skelton Glacier — a 160-kilometre climb up from sea level to 2500 metres with a formidable mixture of crevasses and wide, apparently easy, but often deceptive, snow slopes, jutting mountain spurs, and sudden violent wind storms with poor visibility, as reported by the dog teams.

Meanwhile, at Scott Base we kept in touch with what Ed's tractor train and the husky teams were doing through sketchy radio reports and observations from John Claydon and Bill Cranfield, who were regularly flying up when the weather permitted.

Life at McMurdo buzzed along, with United States Airforce Globemasters flying in, ready to resume airdropping supplies to the South Pole station for the following year, accompanied by Navy Neptunes and Dakotas destined to carry human cargo.

We were diverted briefly from more serious events when Pan American Airways (Pan Am), then the biggest airline in the world, pulled off a great publicity deal by contracting with Operation Deepfreeze to fly one of its giant Stratocruisers (similar in many ways to the Globemasters) on the first commercial flight to the Antarctic, arriving at McMurdo on 16 October.

Pan Am carried 37 passengers — officers and men of a mobile construction battalion and some civilian technicians — and a crew of nine including, to great excitement, two air hostesses.

Displaying a great flair for public relations, United States Navy ensign Morton Beebe, whose principal job was to keep us newspaper reporters happy while gently herding us around, announced that Admiral Dufek would meet the hostesses with American dog teams, that a New Zealand dog team would also arrive from Scott Base and, if possible, a flock of penguins. As the nearest rookery was 40 kilometres away, they didn't, in the event, turn up!

The two hostesses, Patricia Hepinstall and Ruth Kelly, were asked to judge a beard-growing contest, and were confronted with some truly magnificent growths that had been cultivated during the winter months, ranging from neat goatees to full imperials and some that made the owners look like frilly lizards. 'My, that's a nice friendly beard,' said Patricia, awarding the prize to Wally Tarr, the New Zealanders' aircraft mechanic.

The polar party ready for departure — the Ferguson tractors and sledges, followed by the Weasel towing the caboose.

While getting ready for departure, someone, for a lark, ignited a harmless smoke flare beside the Weasel.

Watching was Sir Hubert Wilkins, who had stayed on in McMurdo to inspect the old explorers' huts. He said he first saw a woman in the Antarctic in 1919 during an Australian expedition to Mawson. 'She was engaged to a member of the expedition,' he recalled, 'and came down on the supply trip to see him. Unfortunately, by the time the ship reached us she had married the captain.'

Much was made over the fact that the hostesses were the first women to visit our part of the continent although there were two women scientists at the Russian base about 3000 kilometres away and British women had wintered-over on the Falkland Islands side in earlier years.

The Stratocruiser took about nine hours to fly the 3800-kilometre last leg from Christchurch and landed on the 1800-metre-long runway built on sea ice four metres thick. It stayed two and a half hours on the ice and the crew, and especially the hostesses,

were a welcome diversion for men who had spent a year or more away from civilisation.

Out on the Ross Ice Shelf, Ed was about to begin the slog up the Skelton, but news reaching McMurdo was scant and our editors were getting tired of largely repetitive stories about miles travelled and delays experienced. Where was the action, they wanted to know!

For nine days from 22 October the tractor team, and Bob and George with the dogs, battled unbelievably difficult weather with bad visibility and crevasses — on one day Ed reported 100 or so — many of which broke under the tractors as they gingerly crossed over. Some slopes, particularly from the Neve, through The Portal and toward the plateau, were very tough indeed with the Fergusons needing all the power that Jim and Murray could coax from the engines.

Ed soon discovered that what the dog teams

often reported as good travelling surfaces were quite frequently proving unreliable for the larger tractors with their heavily loaded sledges — huskies crossed unseen crevasses without trouble and liked soft snow, while the tractors regularly needed to be dug out.

All of us in McMurdo, including expedition members at Scott Base, were unaware of most of this in any detail, because the intermittent radio reports were very brief and the aircraft could not fly.

The previous summer of 1956–7, I had hoped I would be able to accompany Ed on this tractor trip, but it soon became very clear that, even if it were possible, I would no longer be a member of the expedition. Also, being on the trail would make any reporter completely ineffectual because of the impossibility of getting stories back to the newspaper.

This became obvious about six weeks later when Doug Mackenzie, from the *Christchurch Star-Sun*, who had taken my place as expedition journalist for the second summer, became frustrated by the lack of news and flew up in the Beaver for a quick visit to get a decent, and much needed, colour story just as Ed was leaving Depot 480. Doug got roped in as a spare driver. He stayed for two weeks, until they reached and began building Depot 700 on 20 December, when he pleaded to return to Scott Base because the New Zealand media were clamouring for the hard news he had been unable to supply while on the trail.

I should, perhaps, explain here that Depots 270, 480 and 700 referred to the number of miles distant from Scott Base. The rough metric equivalent would be 435, 770 and 1120 kilometres.

The core of the Old Firm was now getting very thin, because there were several changes in personnel, forced by a variety of events.

While they were building and stocking Depot 270 Peter flew back to Scott Base for a few days to work out some problems with the radios. Ron, too, was anxious to get back to his IGY work so Ed took

To give the huskies a run, Bob and George initially accompanied the tractor train on to the Ross Ice Shelf.

the opportunity to fly back with him to Scott Base for a brief visit to sort out other expedition logistics and events.

Then Murray Ellis strained his back quite badly after an accident when Harry, travelling with one of the dog teams, arrived at Depot 270 and backed a tractor over him! He was also flown back to McMurdo to be treated at the American hospital and would not return to the Plateau until the tractor team reached Depot 480, a fortnight later.

Ed was now getting acutely short of competent tractor drivers who were not involved in other IGY activities to take on the next stage. He decided he must have Derek Wright, my old cameraman

friend from the National Film Unit, who was still in Christchurch waiting in vain for a flight. George Dufek once more came to the rescue: a quick word in his ear and Derek was on the next Globemaster flight south.

The weather around the Skelton and on the Plateau was also playing up badly and the Beaver, piloted by either Bill or John, made several unsuccessful attempts to get up to Depot 270. Finally, on 7 November, the weather cleared and Peter returned to the Plateau. The following day the two dog teams with Bob, George, Harry and Roy set off to blaze the trail to Depot 480.

But near disaster struck, again, when Peter

slipped while fixing the ventilation on the roof of the caboose and fell heavily on a sledge, breaking three ribs.

On 10 November, the Beaver again managed to thread its way at last through breaks in the clouds, flying Ed back to the Plateau and evacuating Peter who was unable to rejoin the Old Firm and make it complete once more until 2 December, during the building and stocking of Depot 480.

On 11 November, Derek Wright and Ted Gawn, who had been keeping the radios working at Scott Base, flew up to join the team. Ted was filling in for Peter and as a merchant navy radio officer he insisted he was not much of a tractor driver.

Wasting no time and conscious of the delays so far, Ed led the tractors off the next day, following as best they could the trail of the dog teams and advice on the condition of the surface received by radio from Bob. Storms and drifting snow meant many of the dog tracks had been obscured but they reached Depot 700 just ten days later, on 15 December, after extremely difficult travelling through what was now regarded as normal crevassed areas.

Three days out from the new depot their Weasel finally gave up the ghost: it was a tough and valuable little vehicle but prone to mechanical problems and, finally, Murray and Jim had run out of spare parts. It was stripped of everything useful and left behind.

We, and consequently the public back home, were all largely unaware of the difficulties happening on the way to Depot 700, except for sketchy comments from the pilots.

Ed had a true mountaineer's way of airily describing formidable obstacles in casual terms, especially in his very brief reports. What Ed had not told us was that the tractor team had been experiencing an utterly wretched time for the best part of a week before reaching Depot 700. They had edged along, fingers firmly crossed, over literally hundreds of crevasses alternating with an unfamiliar, humped ice surface.

A dozen times a Ferguson or a sledge heavily laden with two tonnes of supplies would gingerly edge its way across a snow bridge, scrambling to get across while opening up a deep, yawning hole behind. Often the vehicles were only saved from plunging through because they were all linked together by a Terylene rope with an eight-tonne breaking strain. On one occasion they nearly lost the caboose and it took about four hours to pull it free.

What we did know was that Fuchs was also experiencing severe difficulties in getting his trans-Antarctic team over to South Ice to begin the crossing in earnest. It now seemed they would not reach South Ice from Shackleton until mid-December at the earliest, about the time Ed would reach Depot 700.

In fact, Fuchs's party reached South Ice on 22 December, taking 29 days to travel the 560 kilometres from Shackleton. They left South Ice three days later, on Christmas Day, and now had 880 kilometres to go, just to reach the South Pole. Scott Base was a further 1900 kilometres away and in a little over two months winter would be closing McMurdo Sound off from the outside world.

Speculation was already gathering strength that, with Depot 700 completed, Ed Hillary might continue on to the South Pole, from where he had been offered a lift home by George Dufek.

Above: *Ted Gawn (left) and Peter Mulgrew were radio operators par excellence and I relied on them to get my dispatches back to civilisation.*
Left: *Loading huskies and sledging equipment on board the expedition's Beaver, to be flown to the Skelton Glacier.*

Naming, or not naming, features

It was not only the Ross Sea Committee that seemed to be oddly out of touch with the reality of Antarctic exploration.

The New Zealand Geographic Board had issued instructions to expedition members that 'no new names are to be attached to features discovered: such features are to be allotted numbers and referred to accordingly by all personnel at the base, upon maps, in all reports and in conversations generally'.

'How bloody silly,' was the general reaction, although Bob Miller put it more politely: 'It is just impossible to put such instructions into practice,' he told me. Bob was not only deputy leader of the expedition but also its chief surveyor and he had been responsible for quite a few new names. Most of the mapping work was done by him, Roy Carlyon and Richard Brooke.

By the time the expedition returned to New Zealand a completely new area of about 55,000 square kilometres had been discovered, surveyed and mapped, mostly around the Skelton Glacier and in the ranges of mountains to the north and south.

Names given by the New Zealanders often graphically described the teams' journeys: Trepidation Glacier, Lower Staircase, Stepaside Spur (where icefalls blocked the way), Halfway Nunmatak (a mountain almost buried by snow),

Dilemma and so many more. One exception was Robyn Peak at the top of the Skelton, climbed by Peter Mulgrew and Harry Ayres. Both men had a daughter named Robyn.

The stuffy instructions from the Geographic Board indicated it would consider suggested names for the numbered features, but they 'must be submitted on the form provided'. The board said it liked descriptive names and it suggested that less common names made a map more interesting, such as Edge, Bottom, Heights, Neck, Scar and Stack.

The board definitely did not approve of 'names that suggested a friendship or relationship, names of contributors of funds, equipment and supplies who by the nature of their advertising have endeavoured to capitalise or gain some commercial advantage, names of products, sledges, dogs or pets'. They warned: 'The ultimate responsibility for the names suggested rests with the administrative authority.'

No one took any notice of these instructions. One slim, tall and very suggestive outcrop in the Koettlitz Divide was discovered by Bill Cranfield, who mischievously dubbed it Gawn after our well-liked and respected radio operator, even though the board sternly said it would not accept names in low taste.

CHAPTER 14

POLAR TREKKING WITH DOG TEAMS

Little that man voluntarily endures is more primitive than living with a dog team, week after week, in Antarctica.

While Ed Hillary and his Old Firm were battling their way across the Polar Plateau on their way to the South Pole, building supply depots for Fuchs, 10 men with the New Zealand expedition spent up to four-and-a-half months during that summer of 1957–58 on the trail with teams of huskies on different trips of exploration, collectively travelling about 5000 kilometres.

Two of the teams spent most of their time exploring and surveying almost inaccessible mountains, glaciers and inlets while the other team slogged for much of their journey through a vast, virtually featureless expanse of snow — except for endless crevasses — with nothing to break the skyline.

In those days, without reliable communication with the outside world, life was dreary and monotonous. These days, after years of space exploration, satellites give instant voice and visual communications anywhere in the world.

Lightweight, concentrated foods have also improved: 50 years ago, breakfast was likely to consist of oatmeal, fatty bacon, a hard energy-efficient biscuit and a drink; lunch would be another biscuit with perhaps peanut butter or meat extract; dinner was pemmican, a biscuit and another drink. Titbits were few and a piece of chocolate a luxury. Dog teams either ate defrosted seal meat, if it could be flown up from Scott Base, or shared the pemmican.

Eight hours is about all a dog team can be worked in a day but in that time they can cover up to 65 kilometres in good conditions. Nine dogs pulling together make light work of a 2200-kilogram load, just as a horse does not feel the weight of a well-balanced cart, once it begins to roll.

A good deal of the remaining time is taken up breaking camp each morning and making it again each night. Tents have to be put up, stores and sleeping gear unloaded from the sledges, spirit stoves lit and snow dug up and put into a pot to be melted for hot drinks. The dogs have to be tethered out in the snow along span lines and fed.

The New Zealanders, each with their team of dogs, had a mixture of skills including geology, surveying and meteorology, and all were seasoned alpinists. Every day, time had to be taken for surveying and geology work as well as keeping a strictly accurate navigation log. Some of the teams also engaged in seismic

Our huskies seemed to love hard work, pulling laden sledges
with a will. Note the bicycle wheel at the back of the sledge,
used to record the distance travelled.

work that meant setting shallow depth charges to determine the thickness of the snow and the height of buried mountains below.

When the sun was obscured — as it is for much of the time by overcast skies — a dead reckoning course was gained by the mileage counter towed behind a sledge. There was nothing fancy about this: it consisted of a standard bicycle wheel with a recorder attached.

A compass was useless, for pretty well all the travelling was between the magnetic and geographic South Poles. Most of the time needles turned crazy gyrations, pointed as far as they were able toward the centre of the earth.

The New Zealand teams each had tiny, light radio sets developed in the United Kingdom and small enough to fit into a pocket. At that time they were still on the military secrets list. Their primary purpose was as an important aid to navigation because they were able to pick up worldwide stations that constantly broadcast Greenwich Mean Time signals.

What is left of the day for a sledging team is normally spent in the tent, writing up diaries, sleeping or lying fully clothed inside a sleeping bag trying to sleep. The stove in each tent is normally left burning each night to raise the temperature a little. With luck, the tent would warm up to about minus 15°C or 32° of frost.

To stop the cold striking up from the snow and ice, each tent had a canvas floor, a sheepskin laid on top and then an air mattress. It was reasonably comfortable.

And to answer the question everyone asks or wants to ask: as far as possible, normal body functions are the final task an explorer performs inside his tent before packing it up and lashing it to the top of the sledge.

At minus 40°C, which also happens to be minus 40°F — it is the point where the two scales cross, a

Strong, dominant lead huskies are a key element in a successful dog team. Several sledgers became so fond of their lead dogs that they fought for permission to take them home once the expedition was over.

common enough outside temperature on the Polar Plateau — breath catches on eyelashes, eyebrows and beard, and turns into ice. On a windy day when the air cuts like a knife, faces can quickly become a complete mask of ice. Strangely, this gives a feeling of protection for a time but sledgers watch each other's faces for the white, tell-tale signs of frostbite.

There are hazards other than the cold: it is almost a given that sooner or later one camps over a crevasse and it happened to several of the New Zealand teams, fortunately without dire results. But, too often for comfort, crevasses gave way while a team was travelling across them and dogs, still hanging from their harnesses, had to be rescued from their depths on several occasions.

Although the teams on the Plateau were constantly among ice and snow there was a great danger of dehydration, for the atmosphere is too cold to contain moisture. It is essential to get enough to drink and this means melting snow. In the tents, sharp, loud crackles of static electricity occur as a person moves restlessly in his sleeping bag, and blue sparks can be rubbed off clothing.

Why do men and now, increasingly, women endure such hardships? One might as well ask why the first Viking sailed into the Atlantic, why Captain James Cook sailed southward into seas that had never been charted or why men now go into outer space. The quest is, of course, for knowledge, driven by an irresistible urge for adventure.

Of the 10 men engaged in survey work during that summer, those who journeyed furthest were Bob Miller from Masterton, New Zealand, and George Marsh, our doctor from Shrewsbury in Shropshire, United Kingdom. George was officially both medical doctor and dog expert but we joked that from the manner he divided his time, he clearly cared more about dogs than he did about expedition members.

Bob and George made what was undoubtedly the longest journey on foot and skis in the history of

Antarctic exploration, longer even than the journey by Roald Amundsen from the Ross Sea to the South Pole and back. But both men insisted that their journey should not be compared with Amundsen's because they had supplies left for them along the way by aircraft and Ed's tractor train, whereas Amundsen had to be self-sufficient.

They were 18 weeks on the trail, sledging 2672 kilometres behind their huskies and walking about 560 kilometres and skiing about 2100 kilometres. They surveyed 38,850 square kmilometres of mountains, glaciers and vast areas of snow — territory that had never before been seen.

Not once did they ride on the sledges that were pulled by two teams, each of nine huskies. They endured temperatures down to minus 67°C, a 110-kilometre blizzard and for 14 weeks were at altitudes above 2400 metres, far longer than any other dog team had ever been. They arrived back incredibly fit but the extreme cold had taken out fillings in their teeth.

Recounting the trip at the end of February 1958, on their return to Scott Base, more than a month after the tractor parties had met at the South Pole, George told how they had first been flown in to the Skelton Glacier Polar Plateau and replenished the depot begun there the previous summer.

Joined by the South Pole tractor team and the dog team making the Darwin journey (see page 102), they then established Depot 480 and had gone on alone to survey the proposed route of Ed Hillary's tractor party as far as Depot 700. When this was done they had branched off eastward to survey the vast area of the Queen Alexandra Range between Shackleton Inlet, the Beardmore Glacier and the 4560-metre Mount Markham.

In an interview with the *New Zealand Weekly News*, George was quoted:

'For the first 300 miles [480 km] *we walked because the snow was too soft for skiing. Most of the journey our*

dogs made great time, averaging 20 miles [32 km] a day and with a maximum of 34 miles [55 km]. We fed them on seal meat.

We ate pemmican. It got monotonous. We tried it with vitamin pills, with curry and with stew. We had what we called a luxury box. Once a fortnight we dug into it. It contained two-ounce tins of anchovies, curry powder, sardines, dates and smoked blue cod.

We were given test packages of food which contained some new type of meat bars, cheese, dried potatoes, dried onions, biscuits, butter, pepper, salt — each food package contained between 5000 and 5200 calories, a man a day.

[We read] everything from magazines to Shakespeare. I had Palgrave's Golden Treasury *and a collection of paperback classics. What occupied us? Mainly the business of the day — how many trail miles we had covered, the performance of the dogs.*

Did they squabble? Definitely not: on the trail they were usually a couple of hundred metres apart and barely exchanged two words. They talked with their dogs, usually about the weather or the dogs' behaviour.

Members of the northern journey encountered greatly different but equally arduous conditions. Leaving Scott Base they worked their way up the frozen, Ross Sea side of the Royal Society Range as far as the Mawson Glacier, seeking access to the Polar Plateau. Repeatedly jumbled icefalls or terrible crevassed areas stopped access up glaciers or

inlets but eventually they decided upon the Mackay Glacier and spent two-and-a-half months mapping and establishing survey stations before turning south, reaching the Skelton Plateau Depot and returning to Scott Base.

The Darwin journey involved accompanying and supporting the southern dog team and tractors as far as Depot 480, seeking a safe route for the tractors toward the South Pole. That accomplished, Harry Ayres and Roy Carlyon then headed east toward the mountains bordering the Ross Ice Shelf. They spent two months surveying the Darwin mountains before safely descending the Darwin Glacier, blazing what was only the fourth safe route through the mountains to the Polar Plateau, after the Beardmore, Skelton and Mackay Glaciers.

In all, the combined efforts of the members of the field parties resulted in the professional mapping of 52,000 square kilometres of the Antarctic. The men, whose feats deserve to be recognised in the annals of great Antarctic exploration, are:

The Southern Survey journey:
George Marsh, Bob Holmes Miller.

The Northern journey:
Richard Brooke, Bernie Gunn, Guy Warren, Murray Douglas.

The Darwin journey:
Harry Ayres, Roy Carlyon, Bill Cranfield, Selwyn Bucknell.

Ready to roll, in jumbled ice at the edge of the Ross Ice Shelf.

Right: *A high-altitude balloon being released. It expanded to enormous size as it rose up to around 24,000 metres before bursting and crashing back to earth. These were essential scientific tools to study the upper atmosphere before high-altitude rockets and satellites were developed.*

Bottom left: *The astrodome at McMurdo Sound, which housed equipment for geomagnetic and upper atmosphere research.*

Bottom centre and right: *This was a weather reporting station that was airdropped in remote areas. After landing, the capsule's legs unfolded to expose a wind vane and instruments measuring temperature and barometric pressure. Information was radioed back to base.*

CHAPTER 15

WHAT THE SCIENTISTS DID

On 3 January 1958, the eve of Ed Hillary's team reaching the South Pole, media speculation was running high and C F Buster Brown, my news editor, was waiting to hear from me. His short fuse blew spectacularly when he received a story I'd written a week or so earlier which began: 'There are four South Poles, not one, and each of them holds scientific keys to the never-ending search for knowledge about the world we live in.'

Was this some ill-conceived joke? Had Lee Martin flipped?

The explanation was much more prosaic: the continual battle to get news stories transmitted on the very limited radio facilities we shared meant that my four-poles piece, which had low priority, was delayed by the radio operators, then finally sent when there had been a slight lull in the heavy traffic. Happily for the news editor, when Hillary and the team finally reached the Pole the real news arrived more promptly.

Fifty years ago we were very ignorant about the Antarctic continent, which was largely unexplored except for a handful of well-documented forays from coastal bases and virtually unseen from the air, so there were scads of stories to write about what the boffins were doing. Even the instruments scientists used were primitive by today's standards. One tool of trade, for instance, was a gravity meter which was lugged around the Antarctic accompanied by a 27-kilogram box containing a complex system of weights and springs.

The New Zealanders' chief scientist, Dr Trevor Hatherton, had one at Scott Base which was flown around the McMurdo Sound region and up on to the Polar Plateau by the New Zealand pilots on their flights in to where Hillary and his men were laying and stocking depots for Vivian Fuchs's crossing party.

The theory behind the meter's box of tricks was simple: gravity's pull changes according to the distance from the centre of the earth, although centrifugal force caused by the earth spinning also tends to make objects heavier as they move toward the poles. Don't laugh — this was serious science at the time.

While I was there a United States scientist, James Sparkman, arrived with a second gravity meter. He was on a world tour, just measuring gravity. Possession of a meter, he told me with his tongue only slightly in his cheek, was a perfect ticket to world travel, although he complained about the meter's weight and that it had to be kept warm electrically. 'No two countries seem to have the same voltages or plug connections,' he said, 'so I also carry about 20 pounds [9 kg] of transformers, resisters and odd-shaped plugs. It doesn't leave much room for luggage.'

Enjoying the sun by one of the melt pools at the foot of a dry valley.

Colonisation is now rushing ahead

At last count eight nations have claimed various wedge-shaped sections of Antarctica, reaching from the coast to the South Pole. Three are clearly defined territories administered through quasi-legal international agreement by Australia, New Zealand and France, and there are at least five overlapping claims by the United Kingdom, Argentina, Chile, South Africa and Norway for other areas.

Some countries, including the United States, Russia, China, Japan, and India, have been very active on the continent, and others, such as South Korea, Germany, the Czech Republic and even Estonia, have established or are planning to build a base or two. Many more are taking part in the 2007–08 Polar Year in some form.

Before the current Polar Year began there were 37 permanent stations in Antarctica and 12 more occupied during the summer months. Colonisation is growing all the time, although there are some pedants who dispute my use of the word, arguing (against accepted dictionary definitions) that colonisation only occurs when fully civilised settlements are established, complete with families, schools and markets.

In all, there are 45 countries that are signatories to the Antarctic Treaty although few recognise the territorial claims of others. Most of these countries, one could cynically say, want to ensure they are inside the tent, not outside, when possible commercial exploitation begins.

But they are at present in general agreement for the banning of mineral exploitation (not exploration) and have established some rules designed to protect the environment that, hopefully, should be effective until 2058.

Main points of the Antarctic Treaty, which has been tweaked and added to several times since 1959, are that it has frozen all quarrels over territorial claims (no new claims can be made and those that have been made cannot be overturned); and created the world's first nuclear-weapon-free zone.

In 1972, the Convention for the Conservation of Antarctic Seals enforced protection of some species and placed controls on catches of others. And in 1980 the Convention on the Conservation of Antarctic Marine Living Resources was supposed to put a stop to large-scale trawling for fin fish and krill although this, like the International Whaling Commission's efforts to ban whaling, has been only partially successful.

The Antarctic Treaty's environment protocol defines the Antarctic as 'a nature reserve devoted to peace and science'. But environmentalists are deeply concerned that the treaty agreements lack long-term solutions and are only delaying, for another 50 years, future rushes for minerals and, more worryingly, drilling for gas and oil.

Environmentalists have an international organisation, the Antarctic and Southern Ocean Coalition, which has an official voice at treaty meetings. In all, there are more than 200 non-government organisations in the coalition that is fighting any regulation of mining in Antarctica, arguing, perhaps optimistically, that it is wrong to even speculate on mining or drilling for oil or natural gas, so it is wrong to attempt to draft a treaty to regulate such activities.

Already there is a big, if underhand, trade in meteorite particles offered on various websites. This seems to have been fed partly by Chinese expeditions that have found thousands of meteorites in at least one mountain range. Treaty signatories agree that all meteorites should go into national collections for scientific study, but this seems honoured in the breach.

One scientist, the distinguished American seismologist and Jesuit, Father Daniel Linehan, measured the height of the South Pole by exploding charges of dynamite near the ring of oil drums that marked the Pole. The seismic echoes indicated to him that the southernmost part of the world was on a rocky shelf 275 metres above sea level, above which was 2498 metres of ice and snow, making the height a neat 2804 metres, but it has been varied since.

Father Linehan had gained fame a few years earlier by directing a sensitive, almost microscopic, seismic excavation of the necropolis below St Peter's Basilica at the Vatican, gradually revealing what is thought to be relics of the first pope.

Jim Sparkman's gravity meter readings at the South Pole left a lot of room for other interpretations, indicating that barometric readings could be out by as much as 600 metres or that there were some 3000 metres of ice and snow below the Pole. I dared to suggest that the gravity meter was unreliable. In the end, there seemed to be general consensus that gravity readings had to be accompanied by complicated continental corrections.

One of the great results of the inaugural IGY year was, eventually, the final compilation of all the seismic studies being made by traverse parties throughout the Antarctic by most of the 64 nations taking part, as well as by members of our trans-Antarctic expedition. This enabled a preliminary map to be drawn of what the land mass of the continent was actually like, buried below great masses of snow and ice.

I wrote a story about this and about how everyone believed the world was round, except for these scientists who were trying to find out just how flat the earth really was at the poles and around the equator. Even sea level is a very loose term because the earth's spinning causes oceans to pile up on some coasts and sink on others. 'It will help immensely the precision of astronomical measurements and of measurements involving a basic network for air

An example of the dry valleys in the mountain ranges on the western side of McMurdo Sound. Some space scientists believed that the surface of these valleys would provide valuable clues about how to travel on the moon's surface. They proved more or less right!

maps,' I wrote. 'And it will tell for the first time how far continents are apart and exactly where certain islands lie.'

That's strange reading now, remembering that Russia's first Sputnik satellite had just begun circling the earth. None of us had any idea how satellites and, eventually, positioning systems would make obsolete so much of what these scientists were doing.

My story about the four South Poles did highlight just what sorts of information the teams of scientists were labouring to discover and just how ignorant we were about the world we lived in.

Studying the geomagnetic South Pole, which is one end of the axis of the earth's magnetic field, was expected to give important clues about what caused auroras, how to manage radio waves for coming space travel and how to improve the way I got my stories back to civilisation. The geomagnetic pole lies about 1265 kilometres from the geographic pole along 110° east longitude. The Russians had just established a

base called Vostok near the geomagnetic pole.

Then there is the magnetic South Pole, more than 2400 kilometres from our South Pole near the Mertz Glacier along 144° east longitude, which the Australian, Sir Douglas Mawson, reached in 1914. The other end of the earth's 9920-kilometre magnetic bar is in northeast Canada.

From a distance, magnetic compasses swing dependably toward this spot and its Arctic counterpart but they become uselessly sluggish nearby. This pole, like the others, shifts constantly and so their positions are continually resurveyed. One difference between it and the geomagnetic pole is that a compass needle above the earth's atmosphere would point to the geomagnetic pole.

The pole of inaccessibility has no counterpart in the northern hemisphere and is the spot most remote from all the Antarctic shores. It is 880 kilometres from the South Pole at a height of about 4200 metres in territory claimed by Australia. There is, as yet, no permanent base there although China is planning to build one. Fifty years ago Russia planned a base to be called Sovietskaya, but gave up. By coincidence, it is diametrically opposite the north geomagnetic pole.

The geographic South Pole is, of course, the best known, although the absolute bottom of the world is not fixed, but wobbles around within that circle of oil drums 100 metres or so wide. It is not even the coldest place on earth — that occurs in the high regions around the pole of inaccessibility, although temperatures below minus 85°C are regularly recorded at the South Pole in winter.

Fascinating snippets of knowledge were being discovered all the time

When living bacteria were discovered in packed snow 28 metres below the South Pole, it dawned upon everyone that the Antarctic was not the clean, disease-free place it was once thought to be. Other organisms had been freely gathered from the air all over the continent.

A physiologist and United States naval doctor, Captain Charles Meyers, dug out the first South Pole bacteria, using immense caution. He slowly sank shafts into the snow, using a collection of ice axes that were continually sterilised, and took personal precautions to ensure he was not digging out bugs he had taken there himself.

The deepest organisms he found came from snow that fell up to 5000 years ago. He isolated these into a variety of cultures, including fungus and mould. A few, he suspected, had sent humans to bed with headaches in very ancient times.

At the same time, living bacteria were also being discovered during deep-core drilling all around the edges of the continent, proving that groups of organisms thrived at temperatures well below zero.

Even near Scott Base New Zealand scientists

established what they called the 1945 layer — a radioactive line in the snow that clearly marked fallout from the explosion of the first atomic bomb only 12 years earlier. And tetanus spores roughly 50 years old were found around Scott's old hut, undoubtedly brought by his party's Manchurian ponies.

Many plant forms, mostly types of lichen, abound in the Antarctic, especially in the dry valleys and — like seeds lying dormant in the desert — it only takes water trickling over the rocks from melting snow to bring them to full growth in rocky soil. Sometimes we found weeds growing in running streams of melting glacier ice, with slime creeping over rocks.

We were constantly being amazed at the way the Antarctic seas teemed with life, as our biologists netted some quite bizarre specimens. Now we were learning that the continent, too, held deep-frozen life forms just waiting for a thaw to be released.

Left: *Admiral George Dufek took a small group of us in two of the United States Navy Otters over to the western side of McMurdo Sound on 31 January 1958, where we made the first ever wheels-to-dirt landings in Antarctica. Ed Hillary and some of his staff accompanied him in one Otter, while we newsmen flew in the other. The previous year Dufek had placed an American team of engineers, surveyors and seismologists at Marble Point on Cape Bernacchi, a rocky but gently shelving finger that pokes into McMurdo Sound from the Wilson Piedmont at the foot of the Wright Glacier, to investigate whether a permanent airfield could be built. They had just finished constructing a 365-metre land strip, the first in the Antarctic. The area is always ice-free and although snow falls or is blown there, it is just as quickly blown away by the winds. Marble Point is about 80 kilometres from Scott Base and about 16 kilometres from Butter Point, the first proposed site for Scott Base. The strip had been bulldozed from the jumbled scoria, marble and granite that makes up the point. The newsmen's Otter had a very bumpy landing and here I am with Admiral Dufek inspecting the broken tail wheel assembly.*
Below left: *A helicopter, an Otter and Neptunes on the bay ice strip.*

Tourism is growing fast

The first wave of tourists began heading for the Antarctic Peninsula below South America, in 1960 but it was about 25 years later before tourism began any real growth. Now it is a huge business with up to 40,000 visitors a year and, according to the International Association of Antarctic Tour Operators (IAATO), growing at an annual 15 per cent, which means there could be up to 200,000 visitors a year by 2020.

What sparked the boom was the break-up of the Soviet Union which left many ice-strengthened Soviet research ships high and dry until resourceful tour operators converted them to tour ships.

Most ply in the Bellingshausen and Weddell seas, south of the Atlantic Ocean and South America, which have reasonably easy access during the summer months, concentrating upon icebergs and the teeming wildlife of seals, penguins and whales. So far, 95 per cent of visits are to a small region, a three-day trip from Ushuaia in Argentina.

A few tourist ships also visit the Ross Sea and McMurdo Sound, cruising along the Australian and French coasts. In addition, there are very popular day, non-stop, charter flights, mostly from Australia and New Zealand, to these coasts after a decade-long halt to flying visits after an Air New Zealand sight-seeing DC10 crashed into Mount Erebus in 1979, killing all passengers and crew.

When the Antarctic Treaty was first signed at the height of the cold war the concept of commercial activities such as fishing or tourism was either ignored or overlooked. In 1991, however, a protocol on environmental protection was added to the treaty and the IAATO was formed, establishing guidelines for sustainable tourism.

Unhappily, membership to the IAATO is voluntary and there is great disagreement among tour operators about what should or should not be done. Tourism companies based in the signatory countries are now required to be certified, which largely means adhering to wildlife-watching guidelines and observing landing procedures at nearly 300 landing sites, as well as, in some cases, carrying a government observer. There are vague guidelines covering where the tourists may go and suggesting that no more than 100 tourists be ashore at any one time. There is no limitation on the size of the ships.

Ed pushes on

Ed, with Peter, Murray, Jim and Derek, reached Depot 700 on 15 December to find Bob and George waiting with the dogs to help build the depot as supplies were flown in. Bob and George also had to stock up on supplies for themselves and the huskies before they headed off on a survey of the mountain ranges to the east.

According to the master plan decided in London three years earlier, Fuchs and his 11 men should have now been coming up over the horizon in their trusty Sno-Cats. But they had not yet reached South Ice, the jumping-off spot for the main trek to the South Pole, and would not do so until 22 December. They were still 880 kilometres from the South Pole and more than 1600 kilometres from Depot 700.

Oddly, Fuchs, in a sparse radio message to Ed a few days earlier, confidently mentioned reaching the South Pole between Christmas and New Year, although this seemed impossibly optimistic when some of us started doing impromptu calculations.

The weather on the Polar Plateau and at Scott Base was again deteriorating — it was bleak with poor visibility — and it was three days before John, in the Beaver, could make the first flight up and begin stocking the depot with fuel and food for the crossing party.

I write, perhaps casually, about flying up, but Scott Base was now five or six hours' flying time away for the single-engined Beaver which had to thread its way through mountain ranges, brave strong winds and climb to 3000 metres or more. Finding the small tractor train on the vast plateau was a skill in itself, depending upon unreliable homing beacons and primitive radar. Every time they flew, the New Zealand pilots were taking considerable risks. A forced landing would have put them in an extremely unpleasant situation.

But, happily for the impatient Ed Hillary, the weather did improve enough for Bill and John to begin around-the-clock shuttle flights, with half-tonne loads of food and 44-gallon drums of fuel each time so that within three days the depot was stocked. Flags were then set on 1.8-metre high cairns, 800 metres apart and spread out for 8 kilometres, to guide Fuchs's party.

Bob and George set off with the dog teams on what was to become one of the truly great Antarctic journeys by huskies, not returning to Scott Base until the end of February after mapping and surveying along the mountain ranges between the Beardmore and Nimrod glaciers.

Fuchs, speaking to a London newspaper from Shackleton a month earlier, two weeks before he set out on a reconnaissance to South Ice, had said: 'The first 200 miles [320 km] are probably the worst terrain

Left: *An example of a bleak, windy day 2500 metres up on the Polar Plateau. The chaps were happy to stay in the warmth of their tent while we unloaded stores from the Beaver.*

South Pole goes commercial

'Civilisation was reaching Antarctica at a pace often hard to keep up with,' I wrote in one dispatch, quoting a message received by the United States Navy in McMurdo Sound from their South Pole base.

On the day that, 45 years earlier, Scott and his companions had reached the Pole after a desperate struggle, the message read: 'Can Hillary and Fuchs use credit for purchases at ship's store when they arrive at Pole?'

Admiral George Dufek assured me, with a straight face, that he had given permission.

we shall have to cross . . . we should like to meet Ed Hillary 1126 kilometres from his base but we shall probably be late and he may have to turn back before we arrive.'

Prophetic words

I wrote on 18 December: 'Ed and his men now have to decide whether they can give fresh support to the British transcontinental group by moving on toward the South Pole.' And I quoted the New Zealand Prime Minister, Walter Nash, saying: 'If Sir Edmund wants to go on to the South Pole and he thinks it is safe enough for him to do so, then I see no reason why he should not do so.' Mr Nash added somewhat patriotically: 'I think it would be a good thing for him to add the South Pole to Everest.'

More cautiously, the Ross Sea Committee, which always trod a safe bureaucratic path, said through its chairman, C M Bowden: 'We are ready to do what is necessary in the circumstances of the day. I don't mean today, but in a few days after communication has been established.'

But Mr Bowden was well aware that he had already sent a message to Ed instructing him not to proceed past Depot 700, which Ed only received after his tractor team had left the depot and were heading for the Pole.

Ed also sent a longer message to Fuchs:

Bunny. Have completed stocking depots as arranged. Left Depot 700 yesterday with three Fergusons and 20 drums of fuel with intention of proving the route out another 200 miles [320 km] *and then, if the going proves easy, doing a trip to the Pole. Did 27 miles* [43 km] *yesterday in heavy going before being stopped by small crevasses.*

Will scrub southward jaunt if vehicles and fuel can be used in any way to expedite your safe crossing either by a further depot or anything else you suggest . . .

A few days later Fuchs replied saying he was pleased Ed was marking the trail further south and asking him to build snow cairns as markers.

Radio contact between Hillary, Fuchs, Wellington and London was extremely unreliable right through this period, partly because the British party were equipped with field radios that were less efficient than the new models Ed had and partly because of severe sun-spot activity.

This meant messages between Fuchs and Hillary, initially almost always in Morse code, had to be relayed through Shackleton, London, Wellington and Scott Base — five separate transmissions, usually over several days! It began to cause quite considerable mix-ups, as replies were often received to messages that were, in the sender's belief, already superseded. And, of course, most of these messages were regarded as confidential.

Later, as both Ed and Fuchs got closer to the South Pole, Peter was able to patch messages through the South Pole radio and for the first time the two leaders were able to cut out the middlemen in London and Wellington and speak directly with each other.

It was actually almost one month later, on the eve of our flight to the South Pole to meet Fuchs, that Ed made public his offer to scrub the jaunt by letting me see copies of the radio messages he received and sent after leaving Depot 700. At that stage the controversy over who said what and who possibly defied who was at its height.

With typical understatement, Ed told me that when the party reached 160 kilometres out from Depot 700, three days after sending the offer to scrub the jaunt, they paused for one full day in case Fuchs made any further request. It was Christmas Eve, and Fuchs was preparing to leave South Ice the following day. He sent a very cheerful, optimistic message to Hillary saying they expected rapid travel from there.

On Christmas Day, the New Zealand tractor team called a rest day, working on the tractors and generally fiddling with their gear. They had what only Ed could called a sumptuous Christmas dinner of salmon cakes, tinned peaches thawed out over a hot air blower normally used to heat the Fergusons' engines before starting them each day, some fruit cake, a small tot of brandy and a cup of cocoa.

Then the original Old Firm initiated Derek as a fully paid-up member, with some ribald hilarity about his love life. I've mentioned Derek was an old friend — we had actually helped build a ski club on Mount Ruapehu together and he was also newly engaged to my first wife's cousin, Margaret. Both were trying to conduct their romance over the very public and restricted radio link to New Zealand via telegrams which, of course, everyone read. They married very soon after we all got back to New Zealand.

When no message came from Fuchs, Ed pushed on another 200 kilometres or so. On Boxing Day 1957, Ed was, in his own words, 'heading hellbent for the South Pole'.

'God willing and crevasses permitting,' he added in the radio message to Scott Base. His decision brought to an end days of uncertainty and doubt and fired up all the other expedition members with new enthusiasm.

Ed's message described a tremendous improvement in conditions on the plateau, although lurking ahead, there were going to be some major problems with soft snow. He said they had been climbing steadily for several days and had reached 2840 metres, deviating westward slightly to avoid two large crevassed areas, and so were now technically running down the small sliver of the French-claimed Adélie Land.

Ed said, in his usual understatement: 'The march two nights ago was the first for some time that we had not seen or fallen into any crevasses. The weather has been good, the wind being almost entirely absent or rising only to a light breeze. The temperature is still

A beautiful summer's day, looking over to the foot of the Skelton Glacier while flying up to the Polar Plateau Depot. For camera buffs, I used a UV filter and shot Kodachrome at 125th on f11.

standing at just below zero Fahrenheit. The party are all fit and well.'

Both the British and New Zealand parties appeared to be free, for the time being at least, of difficult terrain. But the general feeling that all was going well was not to last long.

Ed's party were 420 kilometres past Depot 700, and 385 kilometres from the Pole, when he was surprised and not a little puzzled to receive a message from Fuchs saying he would now like an extra depot laid — Depot 800 — as a precaution. For the first time, Fuchs expressed worries about his fuel supplies and the mechanical reliability of his Sno-Cats.

Ed told me he had to refuse: 'We were now past the point of no return, carrying only the minimum fuel and food I had calculated were necessary to get to the Pole.' But Ed did reassure Fuchs that he was confident the New Zealand team could later boost the fuel supplies at Depot 700 and the other depots as well, if necessary.

Ed points out in his personal account of the crossing that an extra eight drums of fuel were flown to Depot 700 as a precaution, but Fuchs's party had more than sufficient fuel for the whole trip and quite a number of drums were left at the depots for possible future use: although the New Zealanders placed 50 drums in total at the depots, only 20 were used by Fuchs, and his team arrived at Scott Base with 16 drums still unused on their sledges.

Pushing on to the Pole, the New Zealanders were now well above 3000 metres and the temperature was decidedly cooler, although the weather was fine and clear.

But the Fergusons were making very heavy going in soft, deep snow which increased their fuel consumption alarmingly. The high altitude also meant a significant drop in engine power and Ed was becoming extremely worried that, with their slow progress, they would not have enough fuel to reach the Pole.

There was a navigation worry, too. I have already mentioned that Ed was a navigator in the RNZAF during the Second World War, and he was now using a bubble sextant which was becoming unreliable because the bubble was growing larger as the liquid surrounding it leaked. 'The thought of wandering aimlessly around in the middle of nowhere wasn't very pleasant,' he remarked later.

With just 95 kilometres to go, deep snow almost defeated them. The tractor treads sometimes dug down 0.6 metres into the snow before grinding to a stop and then the tractors had to be laboriously dug out with spades. They were now at 3275 metres, and had travelled only 35 kilometres in the previous 12 hours. Hard work at that height was making both tractors and men very weary.

'At one time it appeared as if the tractor train had reached the end of the road,' Ed recounted when speaking to Scott Base by radio on 31 December. 'Deep-bottom snow proved too much for the tractors and they bogged down again and again. Our main worry is fuel, but we are just holding our own.'

There was nothing for it but to strip their load to a minimum and press on.

Talking to Ed by radio the day after he reached the South Pole, he told me that they had to dump one-and-a-half tonnes of supplies: food, cooking fuel, sledges, spares for the tractors and even emergency tents and camping gear, 'and a great many other boxes of equipment'. Everything except what was vitally needed, and even then, the tractors were only capable of a few kilometres per hour.

They slogged ahead and on the morning of 3 January, during a rest break, they were able to make their first voice contact with Fuchs, who told Ed that his party were 600 kilometres from the Pole but was hitting very heavy sastrugi — a series of low, irregular ridges on the snow surface formed by wind erosion — which was delaying them badly.

Ed was continuing to worry, as it turned out

unnecessarily, that he had made some navigational errors — but they started up the tractors after the radio chat and a meal and moved on, keeping a very sharp lookout for the South Pole station. Then, around 8 p.m., Ed thought he saw through some drifting ground fog a black speck ahead and slightly off their course. He dragged out his binoculars: it was a flag and, moving forward, they soon came across a whole line of flags.

They had reached the Pole! By Ed's dead reckoning they still had some way to go, and he guessed that they had probably reached the airstrip. In fact, the flags were markers and they still had about 28 kilometres to go.

Utterly weary, Ed called a halt. Murray, Jim, Peter, and Derek unanimously agreed with him that they should pack it in and get some rest before rolling in to Amundsen–Scott Base in style the following day.

But first, before crawling into his sleeping bag, Peter called up Scott Base, which was keeping an open-radio listening-watch, said, cryptically, 'Rhubarb', then switched off and went to sleep.

Rhubarb, Peter told me later, meant 'have Pole in sight'. It was one of a series of code words devised by the Ross Sea Committee to prevent competing media from getting a jump on *The Times* and BBC, who had helped finance the expedition.

But the message that was excitedly sent on by the Ross Sea Committee, after being relayed to Wellington, was that the New Zealand team had got there. All the competing media could do, one day later, to justify being comprehensively, if falsely, scooped by faulty information was to explain to readers the error.

Ed and the team, after a good sleep and sketchy breakfast, set out at 8.30 the next morning, Saturday 4 January, and by midday they could see the large dome of the South Pole station on the horizon. Dr Vern Houk and Major (Moggie) Morgensen, the co-commanders of the base, came out to greet them

Sastrugi caused by high winds along the glacier. Fuchs's party had little trouble descending the Skelton Glacier from the Polar Plateau thanks to the trailblazing of the New Zealand tractor and dog teams.

in a Weasel about 12.30 p.m. and at 1.10 the New Zealanders pulled into the 'parking lot' at the base and switched off the Ferguson engines.

The Old Firm had begun the 2000-kilometre trek 12 weeks earlier with three Fergusons, a Weasel, the caboose and seven sledges loaded with supplies. They arrived with the tractors and caboose and just two sledges carrying some general gear and half a drum of diesel fuel — 'sufficient for about 10 to 15 miles [16–24 km]. We were cutting it rather fine,' said Ed.

The tractors were to remain at the Pole. After being fully restored with spare parts flown from New Zealand, they were used by American scientists during the next two or three years to range up to 500 kilometres from the Pole on seismic and geology studies.

For now, though, there was the luxury of catching up with civilisation, South Pole style. First thoughts, after weathering the huge reception by everyone at the station, were for hot showers and a decent hot breakfast which, American style, included baked beans and hot dogs.

The Old Firm were genuinely surprised at the congratulations that were pouring in by radio from around the world and the references to being only the third group to reach the Pole by land. 'Scott and Amundsen did it the hard way,' Ed insisted. 'But it's nice to see new faces and have some different company.'

Later, to questioning, he described the long haul as being less strenuous than climbing Everest for the first time, 'but,' he added, 'crossing the crevasses between Depot 700 and the Pole was more nerve wracking than Everest'. And when asked why he pressed on to the Pole replied: 'Because I wanted to. Some people have to have a scientific reason. Not me.'

Now it was over

Well, actually it wasn't over. Little did Ed and his men realise that, from here on, they were about to be swept up in a worldwide media uproar of controversy, compounded by ineptitude, misinformation and confusion from the New Zealand and London committees.

The groundwork for the controversy was laid while Ed was still 95 kilometres from the Pole and Fuchs 480 kilometres away. The London headquarters of the expedition declared, unprompted, that there was no Race for the Pole, before anyone had seriously suggested there was.

The listening media ears pricked up.

Then, the day before reaching the South Pole, Ed sent a long confidential message to Fuchs saying that he was very worried about the serious delays the British crossing party were experiencing and the bad weather and low temperatures they could expect after leaving the Pole.

He described the severe crevassed areas he had experienced and urged Fuchs to consider wintering his vehicles at the South Pole, flying out courtesy of Admiral Dufek, and then returning the following summer to complete the journey. 'This plan would enable you to do a far more satisfactory job of your seismic work,' he added.

'Sorry to strike this sombre note, but it would be most unfortunate if the sterling work you've put in to make your route through to South Ice and the Pole should all be wasted by the party foundering somewhere on the 1250 miles [2012 km] to Scott Base.'

The Antarctic is a desert, with snow so dry it cannot stick to steep mountain sides. This shot in the Royal Society Range shows how the geological and mineral nature of many mountains is exposed.

Ed also copied this message, confidentially, to the chairman of the management committee of the expedition in London, Sir John Slessor, and to Charles Bowden in Wellington, chairman of the Ross Sea Committee.

The morning after Ed arrived at the Pole, Sunday 5 January, he received a reply from Fuchs: 'Appreciate your concern but there can be no question of abandoning journey at this stage.' Taking a very stiff-upper-lip stance, Fuchs added: 'In view of your opinion that late season travel is an unjustifiable risk I do not feel able to ask you to join us at Depot 700 in spite of your valuable local knowledge.' He went on to say that the British would 'wend our way, using the traverse you leave at the Pole'.

Ed, naturally, had no intention of abandoning the New Zealand commitment to see Fuchs and his men home safe at Scott Base and he made it crystal clear that he would join Fuchs at Depot 700, as planned.

None of this frank exchange of views would have become known, had it not been for another slip up by the Ross Sea Committee. Ed's confidential message was, in Bowden's words, 'inadvertently mixed up with a number of press messages' and distributed to the media back in New Zealand who were clamouring for any news about the crossing parties.

Ed, now back at Scott Base, was more blunt when talking to me: 'I was deeply shocked when I found it had been batted around in the press,' he said. 'As far as I was concerned it was purely a private matter between myself and Dr Fuchs.'

The waiting media jumped delightedly, of course, on this rift between the leaders — there was very little else to report on the progress or otherwise of Fuchs party. Vivian Fuchs, unlike Hillary, was tight-lipped, almost secretive, about his progress.

Therefore, commenting largely from a position of ignorance, leader writers and columnists took sides.

Sadness 'at the sight of these two great men quarrelling,' was the theme of the *Daily Sketch*, now long gone from the London scene, while the *Yorkshire Post*, always good for a serious quote, added cautiously that 'without the kind of knowledge no layman could possess it was impossible to form a sound independent view of whether it was right for Dr Fuchs to continue'.

In Sydney, though, *The Sunday Telegraph*'s London correspondent had no doubts, calling Ed's advice 'a deplorable breach of discipline which could endanger the whole enterprise . . . distasteful elements of drama and personal glory are being introduced into what is primarily a scientific enterprise.'

But *The Guardian* saw something else: 'What with sputniks . . . and hellbent for the Pole . . . the International Geophysical Year has already established itself as a successful public entertainment. People are now wondering what other and possibly more spectacular rabbits will be produced out of the scientific top hat before the IGY ends.'

The Times took the same view that I did in *The Daily Telegraph*, telling readers Ed had not only the right but also the duty to urge his opinion regarding the risks entailed in continuing beyond the Pole with autumn drawing on. 'Sir Edmund, though a subordinate, had been properly entrusted with a large power of initiative. His individual thrust to the Pole was quite legitimate as he had done his duty in providing depots according to the general plan.'

And *The Sydney Morning Herald* dismissed suggestions that Ed had neglected his job for personal glory as 'just plain silly . . . he did his job and did it with such efficiency that he found himself well ahead of schedule. It was only then that he decided with the concurrence of Dr Fuchs and the Ross Sea Committee to go on to the Pole.'

The controversy, with anybody and everybody putting in their two-bobs' worth, ranged on and did not quieten down until we flew to the South Pole to meet Fuchs, almost a fortnight later.

Bowden attempted to repair the damage by reassuring everyone that the Ross Sea Committee had never lost sight of its primary duty to support Fuchs, but only succeeded in making it obvious they were not fully in touch with what was going on by adding: 'I'm sure that Sir Edmund also has that responsibility clearly in mind.'

Sir John Slessor attempted a last word, spoken in the old heroic, if confusing, style:

I think they will make it and if there were any prospect of disaster we should tell them to get out. But these are not the days of Captain Scott when there was nothing but gallant hearts, flat-feet and dogs. There are aircraft available, and in this matter the Americans are being very good. Everyone knows there are hazards to be faced but a lot of scientific work has already been done.

It was now 10 January, and Fuchs's party were having a rest and maintenance day, 385 kilometres from the South Pole and about 2355 metres up on the Plateau, right on the edge of a very bad belt of sastrugi.

It would be nine more days before they reached the South Pole during which they would abandon two more vehicles, a Weasel and the Muskeg, and another sledge, leaving four Sno-Cats and a Weasel to haul 22 tonnes of supplies.

Jim Bates and Murray Ellis kept tractors moving

The crow's nest erected on a trailer towed behind the Hillary team's lead Ferguson tractor, designed to aid navigation in poor conditions, was soon abandoned as quite impractical. Visibility from the crow's nest was little different from what the driver saw.

The contribution Jim Bates and Murray Ellis, foundation members of Hillary's Old Firm, made toward the success of the Ferguson tractors' long, taxing journey to the South Pole cannot be overestimated — although it tended to be overlooked in the worldwide drama of the Race to the Pole.

Jim Bates was a lean, earnest garage owner from Morrinsville with fresh ideas and plans constantly bubbling up in his mind. Impossible was a word he did not understand although he worked under conditions others would find impossible.

Murray Ellis, from Dunedin, was a great foil: a heavily built engineer with the technical knowledge that could accept and evaluate Jim's ideas, bring them under control and then join him in the task of making them work.

In the early days of building Scott Base when the four Fergusons were being forced to keep up an around-the-clock schedule hauling all our gear, supplies and hut components between the supply ships and the shore, these two kept the tractors running.

They had no comfortable workshop, so they worked in a large packing case, welding broken tracks and tuning engines that were being driven to the utmost, usually in sub-zero weather.

Often the winds howled around their packing case and it was all their numbed hands could do to hold the ice-cold spanners. Jim got a reputation for forgetting meals, so intently did he focus on the problems. Once he arrived for lunch and found the rest of the camp sitting down to dinner.

Once the pressure eased slightly, we at Scott Base noticed Jim and Murray at work with mysterious lengths of steel they had souvenired from goodness knows where. They welded girders and before long there was a brand-new completely unexpected building, a garage on which someone stuck the notice 'Bates & Ellis, Ltd'.

During the first winter they worked in the garage, modifying or designing equipment for the tractor train journey to the Pole. The caboose, Ed's caravan, was built there with enthusiastic help from Hillary, also a handy man with tools. And they built heated cabs for the tractors so the drivers would be protected from the bitter winds.

Murray was driving one of the Fergusons when the train left Scott Base, while Jim had temporarily to stay behind to look after the base power plant and handle the mechanical problems that cropped up each week. When his relief arrived from New Zealand Jim immediately flew up to join the train on the Skelton Glacier. For a keen mountaineer who thought nothing of sleeping out in an ice cave on New Zealand mountains, there was no better reward.

FLYING TO THE POLE

During the evening of Friday 17 January 1958, three days before Vivian Fuchs and his party were expected to arrive at the South Pole, Rear Admiral George Dufek called me around to his Quonset hut at McMurdo Sound for a drink. By this time we were old friends, having first met in 1955 during the early days of Operation Deepfreeze.

George was a brilliant tactical leader who liked assessing other opinions and it soon became clear he wanted to run past me and his aide, a laconic New Yorker, Commander Merle MacBain, his thoughts about the problems of flying the small press party to the South Pole to witness the meeting he and Ed Hillary were planning with Fuchs. He had already talked to Ed Hillary over lunch earlier in the day and their trip was quickly known to us.

George Dufek had been harassed for the past week by the small media contingent that had flown into the American base at McMurdo Sound. All of us wanted to fly the 1250 kilometres or so down to the South Pole for the meeting — a major exercise for the United States Navy, fraught with danger.

Flying around the Antarctic was, and still is, a risky business and landing on the 2760-metre-high Polar Plateau at the Pole was always difficult.

There had been several crashes, near crashes and a number of forced landings around the Antarctic continent during the past two years. In addition, aircraft regularly experienced engine problems — oil leaks and mechanical breaks — because of the extreme cold. If that wasn't enough, there was always the possibility of getting locked in by the weather: a tiresome nuisance if the small South Pole station had to accommodate and feed a dozen extra guests; and a catastrophe if an aircraft was forced down in the icy wastes.

Naturally, I did my best to wave all these difficulties aside by pointing out to George the bollocking he would get from our handful of the world's press if he and Ed went in to the Pole without us. With some reluctance George agreed to call a meeting next morning, 18 January, where it was decided we would leave for the Pole later that day.

Besides myself, representing both *The New Zealand Herald* and *The Daily Telegraph* in London, there were a number of American journalists who had been reporting on the United States Navy's Operation

Two Neptune aircraft being readied on the sea ice strip at McMurdo.
Behind them is a Douglas DC3.

Deepfreeze from the early days, including Bill Hartigan, the very funny Irish American with the NBC, the elegant Bernie Kalb from the *New York Times* (he naturally bought his cold weather clothes from Abercombie & Fitch in New York) and Saul Pett, a very hard worker from Associated Press.

There were also a couple of New Zealand journalists and two Londoners who had only recently flown in: a dear old friend, Bertram Jones from the *Daily Express*, and a photographer from *The Times*, Stuart Heydinger, who distinguished himself by getting drunk and argumentative the night before the flight to the Pole when most of us were involved in an impromptu party. He was nearly off-loaded by the Admiral. He redeemed himself by taking elegant pictures of the meeting between Hillary and Fuchs.

Noel Barber of the *Daily Mail* was also there.

Through bad luck, Derek Wright missed out on the trip because he had been instructed to get footage of *Endeavour*'s work in McMurdo Sound and could not get back in time. Derek's documentary of the trip is an epic. Quite apart from his news clips, we joked that he was the only man to walk backwards to the Pole — as he was in front of the advancing party, filming their progress.

The weather reports were for fine weather at the Pole, and three ski-equipped Neptune aircraft — small United States Navy fighter bombers with a high power–weight ratio which made them suitable for landing and taking off at the South Pole's altitude in minus 40°C temperatures — were waiting for us. We eventually took off around 4 p.m.

Probably because of my friendship with Ed Hillary, I'd wangled a seat on the same aircraft with him, George Dufek, the admiral's aide and some others. We crowded together on uncomfortable seats in the long narrow Neptune fuselage wearing heavy Antarctic clothing. There was no heating. The Neptunes were faster than Dakotas but the trip would still take the best part of five hours.

The flight took us roughly over the same path that Scott and his four companions had taken in the summer of 1911–12 — due south across the Ross Ice Shelf to the Beardmore Glacier with the spectacular Royal Society, Britannia and Queen Alexandra ranges rising to nearly 3900 metres on our right, dominated by mountain peaks such as Markham and Kirkpatrick.

I had flown a similar trip once before, in early 1957, accompanying Ed Hillary in a Globemaster on a supply flight to the Pole. On the return trip we had flown over the Polar Plateau on the western side of the mountains so that Ed could survey his proposed land route on to the Polar Plateau, up the Skelton Glacier.

In the lower-flying Neptune the beauty of the mountains to our right was awesome, some trailing long streamers of cloud, sitting in icy magnificence. A few of the mountains showed 300 metres or more of exposed rock, vividly coloured by stripes of minerals in rusty reds, oranges and blacks.

After a couple of hours we reached the Beardmore Glacier, which rises from the Ross Ice Shelf about 2500 metres to the Polar Plateau, and as we gazed down at the horribly crevassed surface we shouted above the Neptune's engines to each other, wondering how Scott and Shackleton, on separate expeditions, had managed to travel safely over its surface.

In less than half an hour we had ascended the Beardmore — a journey that took Scott and his men almost two weeks. Then came the long run in to the South Pole from Mount Hope on the edge of the glacier, which Scott had climbed in 1911 to confirm that the glacier led to the plateau. The Admiral's aircraft was still leading, with the other two Neptunes close behind.

Now we were flying steadily across kilometres of an unending plateau of snow and ice, almost like the desert heart of Australia, endlessly streaked by the wind in long lines of sastrugi. Here the plateau was

Above: *The Amundsen–Scott South Pole Station had not yet been covered by snow drifts when we visited a little more than one year after it had been built. On the left of the photo is the emergency tent where we visitors slept.*

Left: *The South Pole, which is about 250 metres from the base, wobbles within this circle of empty fuel drums. The American and United Nations flags fly there, near a small shed that is there for shelter, should a sudden whiteout blow up.*

more than 3000 metres high and we were flying some 5–600 metres above. Because the Neptune cabin was unpressurised we tended to doze on and off in the rarefied air until finally we began to descend and could see the 50-metre-diameter circle of empty oil drums placed by the Americans to mark the Pole.

Before we landed, we flew on some 50 kilometres and sighted Fuchs's Sno-Cats slogging steadily along in what looked to be easy snow, with his two dog teams running alongside. Strangely, we thought, only one figure popped out of one of the vehicles and waved at us.

Then, because the conditions at the Pole were not as favourable as it seemed, our Neptune made five cautious passes over the landing strip after we returned to the South Pole, each at a slightly lower altitude, before we finally touched down. The following Neptunes landed equally cautiously behind us.

In my diary I recorded:

The flight in is always hazardous, and the pilots hate the trip although there is always a lot of bravado about 'the bus ride'.

I guess there are a lot of people who think that all there is to going to the Pole is to catch an aircraft, but it is not so, even though flying is certainly not as romantic or as tough as trekking in by land. The people at the South Pole are living on the edge of danger all the time. It only needs a fire during the winter months to wipe them all out. They are very brave people.

Understandably, the men who would be wintering there seemed pleased to see us all and we were shown to a large canvas tent that had been erected about 100 metres from the two-year-old, and partly underground, United States base as a permanent emergency shelter in case the base was destroyed by fire or some other calamity.

Ed Hillary and George Dufek were given VIP bunking inside the South Pole Station with the 20 men then stationed there, including the chief scientific officer, Major Palle Morgensen, and Lieutenant Vernon Houk, a young navy doctor who was also military commander of the base.

'Great God, this is an awful place and terrible enough for us to have laboured to it without the reward of priority,' Captain Robert Falcon Scott had written in his diary on 18 January 1912, the day after reaching the Pole with his four companions and finding that the five-man Norwegian team, led by Roald Amundsen, had arrived there the previous month, on 16 December.

Exactly 46 years later, we were welcomed at the South Pole by a sparkling, crisp, minus 20°C day with only a light breeze that added almost nothing to the chill factor. Now there was an established base, even if it lacked almost all the comforts of home, with often unreliable communications with the outside world.

But at least the terrible isolation was conquered. It was hard to imagine just what those ten early pioneers had experienced. I could not help but reflect on the fact that once something is achieved it soon becomes commonplace, whether it is breaking the four-minute mile, climbing Everest or reaching the South Pole. As I write this, reaching the South Pole has become almost routine, certainly by much stronger aircraft than we had, and even by adventurers who prefer to walk, including Ed Hillary's son Peter.

The Pole, I wrote in my diary at the time, is a wonderful place but there is a very real feeling of remoteness, of literally being at the end of the earth.

Left: *A glacier tongue feeds down to the Ross Ice Shelf.*

Dufek's pioneering flight

I've already mentioned in an earlier chapter how Rear Admiral George Dufek pioneered a new era of Antarctic exploration by planning and leading the first successful aircraft landing at the South Pole a little more than a year before Hillary and Fuchs reached there.

It is worth recounting in more detail.

A bluff, tough United States Navy seaman, aviator and submariner, Dufek opened up a new age of scientific exploration and colonisation.

Less than two years before we arrived, the South Pole was still one of the world's most remote places. It had been left unvisited since Scott and his party reached the South Pole on 17 January 1912, a month after Amundsen and his

men. It had been viewed from the air on just a handful of occasions.

Dufek became only the eleventh man to stand at the bottom of the world — and the first since Scott — when he stepped from his Douglas DC3 aircraft, called *Que Sera Sera*, on 31 October 1956, after a landing fraught with peril.

They landed at precisely 8.34 p.m., Dufek recalls in his book *Operation Deepfreeze*, and as he jumped to the hard-packed snow 'the bitter cold struck me in the face and chest as if I had walked into a heavy swinging door. The temperature was minus 58°F [minus 50°C].'

The six crew with him brought the number who had been to the bottom of the world up to a grand

total of 17. They stayed there 49 minutes before the pilot, Conrad (Gus) Shinn, revved up the engines, which had remained running throughout, for take-off and nothing happened. The skis were frozen to the icy surface. Shinn had to fire, successfully, all 15 JATO rocket bottles before the aircraft shuddered free and staggered into the air.

The tough little DC3 was also variously known by the military as Dakota, C47, Skytrain or R4D. Equipped with skis and JATO bottles strapped to its fuselage, it could have been designed for Antarctic flying, opening up vast areas.

Since Scott's tragic expedition in 1911–12 there had been little interest in the South Pole, although the American explorer, Rear Admiral

Richard Byrd, United States Navy, had led a privately financed expedition during 1928–30 to the Bay of Whales, the site of Amundsen's base from which the Norwegian led the first party to reach the Pole in December 1911. From there Byrd had made the first flight over the Pole, in a Ford 4-AT tri-motored monoplane piloted by the Norwegian Bernt Balchen, just 27 years before Dufek landed there.

By Christmas, 1956, only six weeks after Dufek landed, colonisation of the Pole was well underway and the permanent population had reached 24, including 11 huskies.

They had all arrived by aircraft except for one marine sergeant who dropped in by parachute, using the unlikely excuse that he was testing why some of the parachutes on supplies airdropped by huge Globemaster aircraft had failed to open. For the record, Richard J Patten tangled in his parachute shrouds but managed to get clear and, unlike the airdropped supplies, landed successfully.

Three adventurers who tried a similar stunt in 1997 were less successful. Americans Ray Miller and Steve Mulholland, and an Austrian, Hanz Rezac, attempted the first group skydive at the Pole but misjudged their height and died when

they hit the packed snow before their parachutes opened.

After the initial flurry to establish the South Pole base in time for the official start of the IGY on 1 July 1957, serious construction continued and exchanges of personnel became routine, if still needing great care.

For a while, we intrepid journalists joked a bit about who was fiftieth or sixtieth in line at the Pole and who had got out of which aircraft first, almost forgetting about Ed Hillary and his team who had made it the hard way, by land, less than a month earlier.

Left: *A Neptune blasting off with all JATO bottles firing, along with its two propeller-driven and two jet engines.*
Right: *The legendary* Que Sera Sera, *the tough and reliable little Douglas DC3 that made the first landing at the South Pole, piloted by another Antarctic legend, Lieutenant Commander Gus Shinn.* (Photo courtesy US Antarctic Program.)

FUCHS AND HILLARY MEET AT THE POLE

We were a motley handful enjoying a sunny, minus 25°C, mid-summer morning at the South Pole on Monday 20 January 1958, waiting with the rest of the world — if our breathless, overheated dispatches could be believed — for the momentous meeting between Sir Edmund Hillary and Dr Vivian Fuchs. After landing late on the evening of 18 January I had spent the next day exploring the base and 'walking around the bottom of the world'.

Some of our party had also tried to earn our keep by helping dig packed snow from an ice tunnel that was then melted to maintain the base's water supply. We also had to sort out an annoying time discrepancy that was beginning to cause all sorts of problems: what day, indeed what time, was it?

This was, of course, mid-summer with 24 hours of daylight, which most of us soon got used to although it bothered the body clocks of some at first. In fact, when travelling on the Polar Plateau it was preferable to move at night rather than day for two reasons: firstly, the sun was in the south, ahead of the teams, which made navigation easier and, secondly, it was slightly colder, which meant that it was technically safer to travel through crevassed areas because the snow should be more firm.

Scott Base, which was directly south of New Zealand, was operating on New Zealand, or Zulu time, as were the Americans because their main base was also in McMurdo Sound. Strictly speaking, however, time at the South Pole, where all the longitudes met, could be anything.

Left: *Fuchs and his team roll in to the South Pole. Sitting on a sledge at the back of the leading Sno-Cat is New Zealander George Lowe, wielding a movie camera.*

Ed Hillary and Vivian Fuchs moments after they greeted each other at the South Pole.

Fuchs, however, was using Greenwich Mean Time. So, when Fuchs's team came up over the horizon it was, to them, late on Sunday night, 19 January, while we maintained we were 12 hours ahead, approaching lunchtime, Monday 20 January. The official meeting at the South Pole was settled amicably when Fuchs agreed to reset their clocks to Zulu time.

As we were watching the British Sno-Cats gradually rising over the horizon, pounding along through heavy snow, they took more than an hour to reach us. They were travelling slowly so that their two dog teams could keep up while the whole convoy deviated around clearly marked no-go snow areas where American scientists were studying the nature of the bottom of the world.

Hillary looked wan, and uncharacteristically had his anorak hood up, covering his head. The mild carbon monoxide poisoning he had received during his trek to the Pole, plus general wear and tear of living for three months on the plateau, had caused him to lose more than 15 kilograms.

He seemed nervous as Fuchs swung down from the lead Sno-Cat, but their meeting was hearty. I moved close to catch their words:

'Hullo Bunny,' said Hillary. 'Damned glad to see you Ed,' replied Fuchs, as the two shook hands.

'I say,' said Fuchs with a British reserve quite typical of him, 'this welcome is rather unexpected.'

And camera clicking went on, with the irrepressible George Lowe rushing around wearing a straw aloha hat and wielding a huge movie camera. Contemplating the media carnival around us, I thought it was more like Hillary meets Fuchs on ice. In all, there must have been about 40 of us milling about.

For the first 10 minutes there was a crazy jumble of disjointed conversation as we journalists fired questions that Fuchs and others tried to answer while the United States scientists and military broke in to congratulate him and wish the party well.

But neither Fuchs nor his men showed any strain of their 1500-kilometre journey and Fuchs made one thing quite clear: 'We're going on.' And that, of course, became the quote on which we all hung our stories.

There was a bizarre moment when, after the British party began opening the first mail they had received since leaving Shackleton base two months earlier, George Lowe discovered he had received an income tax notice.

Later, as we journalists were frantically writing our stories, we did not forget to note that the party were treated by the Americans to a lunch of hamburgers, creamed corn, spinach, diced potatoes and a very large cake with red, white and blue icing. There was bourbon and beer, too, broken out for the occasion — but most of the crossing party preferred to drink coffee or tea.

Fuchs's diary gives a graphic description of the morning:

It took us some time and seven miles [11 km] to find the barrels and line of flags which marked the route in. As the party moved toward the Pole I looked back and thought our convoy a brave sight: the orange Cats and Weasel, together with the loaded sledges bearing many fluttering flags of different colours . . . above all this the great condensation plumes streaming away from the high, open exhausts of the Sno-Cats . . .

As we approached nearer we could see quite a crowd, in fact over 30 people all armed with cameras. These included Admiral Dufek, Ed Hillary . . . the reporters and all the base personnel.

The strange case of the unmentionable media

Fifty years ago, it was quite common for reporters and cameramen to be anonymous, their stories written and their pictures taken as though they were not there at all but somehow reporting through a strange osmosis, rather than actually being an important part, what occurred.

I've already mentioned that we journalists joked that Derek Wright was the first man to walk backwards to the South Pole — a wry comment on that fact that although he was recognised as one of Hillary's team there was a curious lack of acknowledgement that if, for instance, tractors were filmed negotiating a dangerous crevassed area, the cameraman had often crossed over first.

This may seem rather odd these days, when even a brief item on radio has a final tag identifying Joe Bloggs or Mary Whatnot as the source, while even quite casual newspaper reportage carries a byline.

In books written of some momentous event by the people concerned there is rarely acknowledgment that reporters and photographers were recording what occurred, and sharing the same circumstances, unless it is to make a disparaging comment, such as Vivian Fuchs's remarks after arriving at the South Pole about 'the press of photographers making it difficult to move about' — even though, in fact, most of the camera-wielding crowd were either his own crew or members of the South Pole station.

Quite often during my involvement with the New Zealand Antarctic expedition I reported events in which I had been involved, but I seldom mentioned my presence because I knew sub-editors would cut it from my copy.

The best example, one that I record in the next chapter and which I later chided Ed Hillary about — without any rancour, I hasten to add — was my presence on the Neptune during our hair-raising attempts to take off from the South Pole.

In Ed's book *No Latitude for Error* I'm not there at all, although he picked up my quote from Merle MacBain about us all observing protocol as we crowded into the back of the Neptune. But then, I wasn't there in the published newspaper story either, even though I had included my presence (as an aside) in my report.

The New Zealand Herald was quite strict about this anonymity, although there was a type of graded identification that was supposed to be understood by its readers. 'Ordinary' stories by staff reporters had no by-line at all, but special events were distinguished as coming, on a graded scale, from either a 'Staff Reporter', 'Special Reporter' (an ordinary reporter elevated to 'special' status!) or, in the case of stringers, 'Our Own Correspondent'.

London was different and there was usually a by-line on top news stories, although quality newspapers such as *The Daily Telegraph* still didn't expect journalists to 'make' the news, in the way Noel Barber did for the *Daily Mail*.

Thus, on the day of the South Pole meeting, my story in London was from 'Geoffrey Lee Martin, *The Daily Telegraph* Special Correspondent at the South Pole', but in Auckland it came from the *Herald's* 'Staff Reporter, South Pole'. Just another member of our far-flung network, really!

Left: *Waiting for Fuchs beside the ring of oil drums marking the South Pole: Ed Hillary, centre, with Moggie Morgensen and Peter Mulgrew.*
Above: *The small media group was also waiting.*

While visiting the Adélie rookery at Cape Royds I took advantage of a quiet moment to knock out a story on my trusty portable Olivetti, much to the interest of the penguins.

FILING PURPLE PROSE

After the initial welcoming crush we reporters crowded into two Weasels and drove madly back to our tent to hammer out on our portable typewriters the first takes of a story, whose telling would go on for several hours.

Filing purple prose was not going to be easy. Radio reception from the Pole was always unreliable and there were schedules to keep. But the United States naval radio operators had managed to arrange special schedules for this almost overwhelming influx of journalists.

We agreed to send our dispatches in 50-word takes and had drawn lots for priority. Fortunately for me, Peter Mulgrew had offered to help the United States naval operators so I handed my copy in to him. What they did was cut tapes with our copy and then immediately transmit.

In the event, writing turned out to be a marathon — literally. It meant hammering out a take on our portables in the tent, racing 100 metres across the snow to the radio shack, and then puffing our way back to tap out another 50 words.

Having sent off our first brief news flashes, followed by colourful pieces of the meeting, limited in total to 250 words as I remember — five dashes across the snow — we had a little break while Fuchs and his party had a wash and breakfast before giving a longer press conference.

I took the time to wander off, casually I hoped, to a contact I'd made in the United States camp. I'd smuggled in a bottle of whisky to the usually dry navy base and had spent some of the previous day negotiating to have one of the navy crew develop the black and white film I intended to take of the meeting. In those days, of course, developing colour film rapidly was quite impossible and, in any case, newspapers did not print in colour.

It had been agreed to send one picture for me to London as what was called a radio photo, relaying it on from a United States naval station on Balboa Heights, Panama. This was regarded then as the cutting edge of communications. A black and white photographic print was attached to a drum rotating in a dark tube that was scanned by a narrow light beam (this was before lasers) and broadcast as a radio signal. It was picked up at the other end on developing paper, rotating at the same speed on a similar drum.

The result was often very grainy, especially in this case where two transmissions had to be made, but the end result was regarded as a sensational scoop.

These days, when it seems that everyone carries a mobile phone and instant contact can be made by satellite almost anywhere around the world or even far into the solar system, it is hard to comprehend just how isolated we were in the Antarctic in the summer of 1957–58.

Ensign Morton Beebe of the United States Navy who shepherded (and fetched for) the media attached to the navy at McMurdo Sound.

When at Scott Base, expedition members were limited to one short call home each week. Those out with Hillary driving hard for the South Pole, or those doing survey work with husky teams in the mountains or on the Polar Plateau, had no contact with home and only brief, limited and scheduled contact with the base.

Nowadays, laptops, modems and satellite communication have changed a foreign correspondent's life forever. A colleague who visited the South Pole base a few years ago, and sent back a colour photograph by laptop on satellite phone to his office with only a few seconds' delay, told me how he then had a 10-minute conversation with the photo editor in London, who questioned the intensity of the blues, while getting the technical qualities just right.

Right: *Inside the press tent at McMurdo Sound.*
Centre: *Noel Barber, of the* Daily Mail, *who was a dab hand at making himself part of the news.*
Far right: *The 'temporary press hut' at the South Pole. We media hacks were housed in this large tent, planned as emergency accommodation should the Pole station be destroyed by fire or other causes.*

Making the news

The legendary Noel Barber, in those days a high profile foreign correspondent for the *Daily Mail*, had characteristically made a whirlwind visit to McMurdo Sound five weeks earlier for one of his celebrated 'I make the news' pieces beloved by his boss, Lord Rothermere. He then flew out, telling us all back in McMurdo Sound the Fuchs–Hillary meeting was now a non-event! He returned, though, when the 'Race for the Pole' got much bigger than even Barber's dramatised exploits.

In a deal sewn up in Washington, George Dufek had agreed to fly Barber to the South Pole base on one of the regular supply flights just after New Year while the rest of us sat in McMurdo Sound and fumed.

Barber was a flamboyant, likeable chap: a damned good journalist, quite cynical and shameless over the way he and the *Mail* went about building headlines and circulation.

Anyway, down in the Antarctic, Barber set about making his own headlines. 'I am off to the Pole,' trumpeted the *Daily Mail*'s banner headline across its then front page the day Barber left on his flight.

But Barber was not only a good craftsman, he

had that essential extra ingredient we all need, called luck. The regular seven-hour flight of the Dakota carrying him to the Pole included stopping to resupply a small weather station at the foot of the Beardmore Glacier. Then they flew on to the Pole but shortly after they arrived there a sudden storm blew up and the aircraft and crew were grounded. The weather was so bad that the station was out of radio contact with McMurdo Sound and Barber could not file any copy.

Unfazed, the *Mail* ran another banner headline the next morning: "Where is Barber?" it asked. Then, the following day, after the storm abated,

their answer was in even bigger type: '**I AM AT THE POLE**', accompanied by a typically *Mail* secondary headline: 'The first Briton there since Scott' — completely ignoring the hard-won achievements of his hosts, the Americans, and those of Ed Hillary and his companions.

But I managed to have a small swipe at Barber that he didn't find out about until later.

Bertie Jones from the *Daily Express* in London had not yet arrived in McMurdo and in a deal with *The Daily Telegraph* that I never completely understood, the *Express*, which was the *Mail*'s hated rival, had arranged with me to write a piece

designed to 'kill' Barber's scoop.

The result was that on the day the *Mail* was trumpeting that Barber was Scott's successor at the Pole, the *Express* ran a full Op-Ed page piece on 'The Bus Ride to the Pole' from me, underneath a very funny Giles' cartoon showing traffic chaos there and a New York traffic cop trying to sort it all out.

Neither my story nor Barber's reflected the truly bleak, inhospitable conditions at the South Pole, of course, but it was all regarded as good fun!

Lift off! The last Neptune to take off before our abortive attempt hurtles off from the South Pole airstrip at 2800 metres, leaving a huge plume of blasted snow in its wake.

CHAPTER
20

A DIFFICULT TAKE-OFF

Ed Hillary grunted 'Stop wriggling' and heaved his considerable frame on top of me. I was thankful that he had lost a lot of weight during the trek to the Pole, but he was still bloody heavy.

Then we both grunted as Admiral George Dufek, large and solidly built, landed on top of him. Underneath me, the admiral's long-suffering aide, Commander Merle MacBain, muttered something about this being a fine example of the United States Navy's priority pecking order.

We four were now crushed into the narrow tail section of our Neptune aircraft, endeavouring to take the weight off the aircraft's nose ski so that it would be easier for the aircraft to lift off in the rarefied air of the South Pole Plateau. Attempting to fly out from the Pole was proving to be even more exciting than the flight in.

Our first attempt at take-off had been aborted when only 12 of the 16 JATO bottles of rocket fuel strapped around the Neptune's fuselage fired as we hurtled down the 3000-metre runway of powdered snow at about 130 kph. This caused the aircraft to swerve into deep soft snow drifts and only the skill of our pilot, Commander Jack Coley, chief of the United States Navy squadron in the Antarctic, had saved us from a nasty accident.

JATO rockets augmented the Neptune's standard, if formidable, two piston-driven propeller engines, plus two jet engines that were used for take-offs or emergencies. The JATO rockets were only used for difficult take-offs or when the aircraft was overloaded — both of which applied to our South Pole departure. 'Two turnin', two burnin', 16 pushin',' quipped the pilots.

Getting back on to the runway, we slowly taxied along to the base where their last set of four JATO bottles was fitted to add to the four that hadn't fired on our first attempt.

Our second attempt was made about half an hour later but it again ended in disaster when only the four new JATO bottles fired, although we damned near made it as Coley kept the Neptune bouncing over sastrugi for about 3000 metres — far beyond the end of the runway.

Now, as we scrambled into the Neptune's tail section, this was the third attempt and because there were no more JATO bottles available Coley had decided to try without rocket assistance, ordering the passengers into the back.

Before I lay down, I'd looked through the aircraft window to see, half a mile away, most of Fuchs's party as well as the United States scientists and Navy personnel at the base standing in a cluster, watching, with cameras at the ready. It popped into my mind that they were probably waiting to capture a spectacular crash.

The Neptune's engines screamed again and, using every ounce of power, we bounced the length of the runway across the snow before Coley shut down the engines for the third time. Unhappily, we had never looked like getting airborne, even though Coley pushed the engines as hard as he dared. So it was back to the base again.

The four of us in the tail section unravelled ourselves and George Dufek went into a huddle with Jack Coley.

Merle MacBain, who had that New Yorker's ability to look immaculate, even in an old and dirty anorak, dusted himself down and winked at me. It looked like we might be stuck at the Pole. Not a bad idea, I thought privately, now that we'd got rid of the other journalists. But I was young then.

We were the last scheduled Neptune to visit the South Pole station before the onset of winter because dropping temperatures made take-offs and landings even more hazardous. The other Neptunes that had helped carry the welcoming party to the Pole had left before us and were now well on their way back to McMurdo Sound.

Admiral Dufek rapidly got on the radio to the Americans in McMurdo Sound and ordered one of the Neptunes in McMurdo to return with more JATO bottles. So, sadly, my hopes of staying with Fuchs and travelling back to McMurdo with him were shattered when, half a day later, a new set of JATO bottles were flown in.

They were strapped around the Neptune's fuselage and after another uncomfortable, hair-raising and very bumpy ride we finally lifted off for McMurdo Sound using every bit of the snow runway. The rescue Neptune also took off without incident. This was not the end of the drama, though.

The regular supply Dakota was due to fly from McMurdo the next day on its last trip of the season and would take out Fuchs's two husky teams, along with Peter Mulgrew who had stayed on at the Pole base to maintain radio contact between Hillary and Fuchs, and that would be the end of visitors to the South Pole station for the summer season. On the way, the Dakota was forced to make an emergency landing about 2200 metres up on the Polar Plateau, just south of the Beardmore Glacier, when its pilot, Lieutenant Commander Gus Shinn, reported an oil leak in one engine. In landing, the Dakota skidded on the icy surface and also damaged its landing gear.

Shinn, who had piloted the first aircraft to land at the South Pole three years earlier, with his four crew set up a tent, confident their survival gear would keep them safe for several days. With the weather holding fine, another Dakota flew to the rescue the following day, repairs were made and the mission to uplift the dogs and Mulgrew was completed.

'This sort of emergency is almost routine, down here,' Commander Coley commented to me, dryly. 'I've been there six times now and not one trip has been uneventful.'

Now aircraft routinely, if still cautiously, land and take off from the South Pole base during the summer months — but in those days the now-obsolete Neptunes and the humble Douglas DC3 were the only aircraft available that were configured to land at the South Pole.

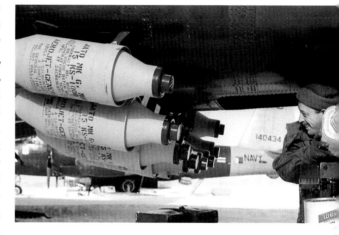

Above: *A closer view of the JATO bottles. Crew are loading packages of ham for the South Pole station.*
Left: *'Two turnin', two burnin', 16 pushin', is how pilots described a Neptune's take-off. The pods at the end of the wings housed radar and navigation gear.*

LIVING AT THE BOTTOM OF THE WORLD

The establishment of a scientific station at the South Pole in November 1956 by the United States Navy was an amazing, audacious, even Herculean accomplishment. Nothing, since the journeys of Amundsen, Scott and Shackleton, had come close in the history of Antarctic exploration.

Yet this great achievement received only scant attention or acknowledgement in a world that was preoccupied with the British and French invasion of the Suez Canal, the eruption of a new outbreak of fighting in the Middle East, and the Hungarian uprising against their communist leaders. Even in the United States, people were focused on the forthcoming presidential election, the uneasy cold war truce and fears of the newly developed hydrogen bomb. New Zealand and Britain were concerned with their own Antarctic endeavours.

Recounting the events much later, George Dufek was laconic when he described what he called his 'quiet victories in the service of knowledge', although I sensed that he felt that the navy, army and air-force personnel comprising Task Force 43 under his command deserved better.

He called the stations they established at the South Pole and elsewhere in the Antarctic beachheads which were built and made ready for the 'occupying forces' — trained scientists whose only opponent would be the unknown.

Following Dufek's landing on 31 October, the second landing at the South Pole was made on 20 November 1956, by two DC3s (R4D aircraft to the navy) that unloaded seven men and 11 huskies. Dufek was, this time, riding in an air-force Globemaster that circled overhead until the landing party set up a camp, before parachuting in several tonnes of supplies: food and fuel, temporary accommodation, a Weasel for powered transport, as well as sledges for the dogs.

It was minus 52°C and the advance party, after determining from ground navigational observations exactly where the South Pole was, moved everything about 13 kilometres and began the task of building the base.

The whole surface, they reported, was compacted snow, not ice, and firm for walking with footsteps sinking in about five centimetres. Aircraft skis sank about 30 centimetres. More importantly, they reported that digging was easy and that there was no difficulty in sawing blocks of snow to be melted for drinking, cooking and washing.

Then the massive airlift by Globemasters based in McMurdo Sound began: three flights a day, each dropping about ten tonnes of supplies when weather permitted. Ten more men were flown in a week later, making only the fourth and fifth landings, and being Americans they took with them three cooked hams for a delayed Thanksgiving dinner.

Above: *This is probably the first flush toilet in Antarctica, perched over a melt stream at Marble Point. In the background is the edge of the Wilson Piedmont Glacier tongue.*
Left: *Feeding a husky team. I captured this midnight sun effect by using a UV filter with my Retina stopped well down.*

'Flying in' sounds laconic, but the tough little DC3s and, a little later, the Neptune fighter bombers, were often operating above their maximum safety margins. On each flight passengers and crew were dressed to expect the worst and aircraft carried survival gear, including sledges, tents, sleeping bags and sufficient food and fuel for crew to make their own way back to safety, along the same routes that, at that stage, only Amundsen, Scott and Shackleton had ever travelled.

By 2 December, flying and working in temperatures still hovering around minus 30°C to minus 35°C, the population at Amundsen–Scott South Pole Station, as they decided to call the base, had reached 24 men. The little permanent village was fast taking shape and only covered tunnels linking the buildings still needed to be constructed. Eighteen men — nine scientists and nine supporting navy personnel — were to stay for the winter.

Prefabricated sections of the station huts had been delivered and only a year's food supply and a large reserve of diesel fuel remained to be airdropped. And that would be the last physical contact with the outside world they would have until the following summer season began. By the end of February the airstrip on the bay ice at McMurdo Sound would have broken up and all the aircraft departed. It would not be rebuilt until the following October, on new bay ice that formed during the winter months.

When Ed Hillary and I flew in a Globemaster over Amundsen–Scott Station on 17 February 1957, airdropping the last of the winter food supplies, the assembled huts, aurora and radar domes were clearly visible from the air and a jaunty orange and black mast with a ball on top, about half a kilometre away, marked the position of the actual pole. In all, about 750 tonnes of buildings, equipment, fuel and food was dropped in three months from these massive freighters.

Ed had arranged the ride with George Dufek,

asking that the Globemaster fly back to McMurdo over the Polar Plateau to the west of the mountain ranges, along the route he proposed to travel the following summer. As a goodwill gesture he took with him a crate of New Zealand eggs which were dropped along with the other food. Later I was able to report that only one egg was cracked, according to the South Pole cook.

As it happened, I was also on the first Globemaster supply flight to the South Pole the following summer, on 17 October, exactly eight months later. As we flew low over the station we could clearly see all 18 men standing in the snow, waving wildly in clear, minus 51°C weather. What was exciting them, I'm sure, was that we were carrying two large bags of mail, to be airdropped along with fresh food. It also meant that within the next six weeks or so most of them would be going home.

The excited voice of Lieutenant John Tuck,

Above: *Marble Point is at the north entrance to New Harbour, opposite Butter Point, on the western side of McMurdo Sound. It was developed by the United States Navy as a scientific base incorporating a small airstrip.*
Right: *Bill Hartigan panning for gold (which was there in minute quantities).*

co-commander of the station, came strongly over the radio: 'You are in sight. You are nice and big and beautiful.'

The cluster of buildings was still as well defined as it had been the previous autumn although snowdrifts were beginning to cover them, blurring the outline of the station. (Three months later, when Fuchs arrived, the buildings were covered even further.) Now, too, we could see the ring of fuel drums taking shape around the Pole.

Our first drop consisted entirely of fuel and

landed about a quarter of a mile from the base. The second, containing the mail, fresh food and other luxury items was spot-on, indeed nearly landing on the Weasel that was racing out from the buildings to pick it up. Later, after we returned to McMurdo Sound, Lieutenant Tuck reported that all work had stopped for the day as they sat reading letters from home and enjoying a late breakfast of southern fried chicken.

Ed Hillary was, of course, by this time leading his Ferguson tractor train up the Skelton Glacier and Bob Miller, the New Zealand deputy leader who was soon to embark on an epic dog sledging trip, was on board the Globemaster with me to have a fresh look at Polar Plateau conditions. As we peered down at the surface from about 800 metres on the return trip, Bob was delighted with what he saw: 'That is good snow for sledging. It looks good for our dog teams.'

Sightseeing from a Globemaster

I arrived back at Scott Base from a flight to the Polar Plateau with Bill Cranfield on 11 February 1957, to learn that the Americans had a place for me on a Globemaster supply drop at the South Pole later that day, so after a hasty breakfast I fell into my bunk for a couple of hours' sleep in my clothes and then hitched a Weasel ride to the airstrip.

We had all been impressed by the size of the Globemasters viewed from the strip, but inside, the huge no-frills cargo hold seemed immense with bucket seating along the sides. It was the first two-storey aircraft, I believe, and during the trip I went up on to the flight deck where there was a small dining room plus a four-holer, four-urinal toilet and a ladies' powder room.

We climbed up to about 4000 metres without oxygen during the flight. The flight crew wore oxygen masks, of course, and there were masks for passengers hanging at intervals along the cabin. Now and again we would go and take a puff or two and it certainly helped combat our tired feeling.

We flew directly south, taking the same route as Scott and Shackleton. Looking down at the great Beardmore Glacier I wrote in my diary:

Those poor bastards . . . the Beardmore looks to be a terrible route, full of crevasses and craggy outcrops although the mountains look old, more rounded and weathered.

The glacier is very wide and the Queen Maud Mountains have some unexpected and attractive colouring, although not in the same class as in the Royal Society Range [where Bill and I had flown earlier in the day]. The Plateau is nothingness. Nothing and nothing for mile after mile. Sometimes it is extremely hard to see the horizon and sometimes there are two horizons — the bottom of the cloud layer and the edge of the cloud shadow on the snow.

The base is one large building with an observatory dome at one end. It is a sort of 'double L' shape, right in the middle of this nothingness, although the surface looks a great deal better than at our Polar Plateau Depot.

We made three drops, all done efficiently and successfully right in the zone near the base.

It is sobering to contemplate that within 24 hours I've casually done what it took Scott two full years to do . . . explore the Polar Plateau and then go in to the South Pole. Scott could never have dreamed of setting up a scientific station there and people wintering over. The continent is being opened up in a way those early explorers could hardly imagine.

The only event of note was the Globemaster's outer port engine caught fire — some problem with the propellers being reversed, and it wasn't serious.

How was the South Pole inhabited so quickly?

How had these hardy Americans made a home, at the bottom of the world, living in a prefabricated environment on the fringe of disaster?

The work programme included constant observation of all the IGY studies: glaciology, aurora and airglow, geomagnetism, gravity measurements, ionospheric physics, meteorology and seismology along with recording just what it was like living at Amundsen–Scott.

They succeeded in carrying out all their work, even though the outside temperature dropped to the lowest ever recorded at that time on the face of the earth, minus 74.7°C. At that temperature two men deliberately went outside and walked around for ten minutes to see what effect it would have on them. Well rugged up and wearing face masks, they reported that, although it was difficult to breathe and they moved rather sluggishly, they just felt cold.

The main living huts were built just as they were at Scott Base, rather like refrigerators, but designed to keep the cold out, not in. There were no windows, because glass is a poor insulator of heat and in any case, who wants to look out at a landscape that is utterly monotonous and never changing. Heavy doors swung shut automatically and oil heaters controlled by thermostats kept the rooms at a constant, comfortable temperature. Fans provided ventilation.

Recreation was limited, naturally, but there was a measure of civilisation: good food, warmth, films every night and the absorption of a fascinating job. A small pool table had been airdropped in, along with an extensive library, a good radiogram and long-playing-record library to suit all tastes.

There were regular work-out programmes: a popular relaxation on mild days was to take a walk around the world, which meant strolling briskly the 40 metres or so to the ring of oil drums in, perhaps, minus 20°C or minus 30°C weather, and doing a circumnavigation. This provoked a constant topic: how does one tell direction, when every direction is north? Residents of the Pole solve this by making direction a matter of degrees — the degrees of longitude that fan out from the spot.

Perhaps the most fascinating study for the South Pole residents was one they took part in every day — working in the ice mine to dig enough snow to provide for their individual needs.

When we flew down to the South Pole to meet Fuchs we could not help but see, as we approached the station entrance, a prominent notice that reminded everyone, without exception, that they had to collect a parachute bag of snow every day from the ice mine to be melted into water. When I was there the mine had already, in one year, reached a depth of 30 metres, angling down at about 18 degrees.

Working at the ice face was exhausting, even though we were all very fit. The slope made both walking down and back again difficult and the temperature was a constant minus 52°C. It was a breathtaking, chilling chore to chip away with an ice axe, taking about half an hour to fill the parachute bag. The notice also reminded everyone that if they wanted a shower an extra parachute bag had to be filled. I certainly didn't feel the need to shower and neither did anyone else at the time.

This pit was also where the study of snow stratification took place, with the snow crystals yielding a valuable history of the Antarctic, bacteria and even pollen dust that gave clues to wind patterns, and minute traces of ash from volcanic eruptions somewhere on earth hundreds of years before. All of these were radiocarbon tested to determine age.

Fire is a constant fear and extraordinary precautions are taken to ensure there will never be an outbreak. Each man is drilled in a particular task, taking his turn at fire warden duty, and there are constant fire drills. When I was staying at the Pole there were two alarms, fortunately both false, but no one grumbled because they knew just how much their lives depended upon absolute precautions.

As visitors, we lived in the small canvas steel-framed hut heated by a small oil stove. It was placed a prudent 90 metres from the main base, which would serve as emergency quarters. At that time, there was sufficient food and fuel stored around this hut to last the 18 men about 10 months. They would not live comfortably but they would manage to stay alive until help came.

Most of the men, when I was there, had hobbies. Lieutenant Vernon Houk, who replaced Lieutenant Tuck as military commander for the second year, grew Californian cotton plants under shelter and in heated soil alongside a miniature garden of cereals and vegetables. He had rigged powerful lights that were switched on and off to simulate day and night.

But to the utter bewilderment of Vern, the cotton seed plants had come through upside down, with some of their roots in the air. His half-serious explanation, when he took me to see for myself, was: 'This is crazy, mixed-up seed from the northern hemisphere! I thought this would help pass the time, but this cotton is driving me nuts.'

Some people would think that volunteering to live at the South Pole was pretty mixed up, in itself.

Two colleagues, Bill Hartigan (left) and Denis Wedrell, at the foot of the Wright Glacier near Marble Point.

CHAPTER
22

SHOOT THE HUSKIES!

There was uproar, starting in New Zealand but moving swiftly right around the world, when word got out that officialdom had decreed the expedition huskies were to be shot.

Remembering the unhappy fate of dogs taken south with Scott and Shackleton, I had written a story saying that both the Ross Sea Committee and the New Zealand Department of Agriculture agreed that the death sentence was the kindest way to deal with the dogs, once the expedition was over.

The Ross Sea Committee, which took very seriously its mandate to administer the region allocated to New Zealand's care, demonstrated again that it had little understanding of public opinion. Nor had it considered the sensitivity of its decision, considering that most of the huskies had been sponsored by school children. It decreed that the huskies would be better dead than living in the 'hot' New Zealand climate and the Department of Agriculture contributed by huffing on about disease-carrying dogs.

The story broke when a New Zealand government cabinet minister made an inspection of Scott Base, courtesy of a flight south with Operation Deepfreeze in October 1957, and was told by Bob Miller and Harry Ayres that they had been refused permission to take their lead huskies back home.

To his credit, the minister's immediate reaction, as I quoted him, was 'what a lot of rot' and he added vigorously that he saw no reason why the huskies could not return. He didn't count on officialdom which immediately took refuge in doublespeak and spin to claim there was no embargo. But in the same breath the Ross Sea Committee and other authorities said they were afraid the huskies could be a danger to children, livestock and other dogs.

'We've grown to love these dogs,' said Bob, reflecting the views of expedition members who said they wanted to take a dog home.

Bob was understating their feelings. Some of these men had lived with these huskies for weeks on end, sharing food and working together in one of the world's harshest environments. They even talked to them in a fascinating mixture of Greenland Eskimo, for commands, and rough English slang.

Newspapers around the world enthusiastically followed up my story. Within a couple of days a Mrs Volney Phifer, of Gillette, New Jersey, had sent a cable to McMurdo Sound via Operation Deepfreeze offering an 11-hectare farm as a permanent home for the whole pack of expedition huskies, which had expanded to 54 dogs and pups.

More savvy to public opinion, the Americans in McMurdo Sound quickly decided their huskies would return by ship when their work was completed, inoculated against distemper and briefly held in quarantine. Most of them would be sold to private buyers.

And in Japan, angry protests by dog lovers forced that country's Antarctic expedition to declare that they were going to save their huskies, too. But it didn't quite work out that way, for them. Their exploration party

Above: *Two of the many young huskies born at Scott Base.*
Left: *A husky team on a training run across the bay ice near Scott Base. Some of the members of the New Zealand team are sitting in the sledge to provide weight.*

was forced to abandon their seven dogs during a fierce storm that forced the early evacuation of their base camp. The story of the huskies' survival during the Antarctic winter was made into a stark but very popular Japanese movie, *Nankyoku Monogatari*, in 1983 and reissued in 1993. It then was made by Hollywood in 2006 into an emotionally charged drama called *Eight Below.*

In New Zealand, confusion about the fate of the huskies reigned for the best part of three months as officialdom said one thing, back-tracked and then said something else, and public opinion grew angrier. Finally, in late January with the trans-Antarctic crossing story nearing its end and the expedition's members soon to return home, the Ross Sea Committee, with a collective straight face, said it had granted a reprieve.

Zoos in Auckland and Wellington would take some, said the committee, and it then transpired that the agricultural department would allow individuals to take dogs home. It would even allow them back in New Zealand without quarantine 'because there is no cleaner place in the world to live in than the Antarctic and the dogs are healthy'.

George Marsh had already avoided New Zealand authorities' to-ing-and-fro-ing by arranging for his lead dog to be sent back to England courtesy of the Americans. But the British authorities were implacable: their huskies that had accompanied Vivian Fuchs as far as the South Pole, and then flown on to Scott Base by the United States Navy, must be shot.

Ed told me recently that he was horrified at the decision but reluctantly felt that he would have to do the job himself before he went back to Depot 700 to join Fuchs on the last legs of the journey.

'I had been given a pistol and ammunition to keep at Scott Base,' he said, 'so I talked it over with Harry Ayres who offered to help me. With a minimum of fuss we took their huskies behind a bluff, a distance from Scott Base, and I shot them one by one. It was not at all pleasant.'

Some of the New Zealand huskies did stay at Scott Base and were used for several years by geological and other field parties.

The husky story doesn't end there, however. Many bizarre things are done in the name of the environment and political correctness and so, some 35 years later, an international forum decided that huskies were to be banned from the Antarctic continent because it was not their natural habitat. The people making that decision obviously did not consider humanity's presence.

Still, their decision was made when the era of huskies and sledging journeys playing a part in polar exploration was fast disappearing as new and less time-consuming types of snow and ice transport were developed. Sadly, most of the remaining huskies in the Antarctic were then shot.

Right: *Harry Ayres, the Southern Alps mountaineer world famous for his ice technique, loading a husky into the Beaver.*
Far right: *A dog team sets off.*

CHAPTER 23

JOURNEY'S END

In the end, Fuchs's journey from the South Pole to Scott Base was something of an anticlimax, even though there were still lingering doubts about their ability to reach Scott Base before McMurdo Sound started to freeze over, forcing the last ships to leave.

They were to battle bitter cold and fierce winds, were forced to drive gingerly through the same crevassed areas experienced by Hillary's team and were constantly held up by mechanical troubles tormenting their Sno-Cats, but at least they were within help from both the New Zealand and American bases. And, if the worst came, they could always winter over in McMurdo Sound.

On 24 January I wrote, accurately but somewhat dramatically:

Fuchs and his 11 men left the South Pole today . . . their enemy during the 1250 mile [2000 km] journey ahead will not be so much the terrain as the deadly onslaught of winter. It was just this that beat Scott and his companions.

Until now Fuchs's party has travelled in temperatures averaging around minus 5°F [minus 20°C]; they can look forward to temperatures as low as minus 40°F [minus 40°C] and numbing winds that blow almost continually across the Polar Plateau as they move further into February. They face days upon days when drifting snow sweeps across their path and compasses cannot point accurately because of the proximity of the Magnetic Pole.

In such conditions man needs only to take off protective outer gloves for a few seconds to have his hand numbed beyond all feeling and suffer minutes of torture as it thaws out again. Frostbite will blotch their faces and hands and leave scars that will take months or years to erase. Already Dr Fuchs's hands are scarred and cracked from working in the cold.

There will be days when Fuchs and his men will not be able to move at all, pinned down in crevassed areas with visibility blotted out by blizzards. But the cold will have one advantage; it will mean that the snow bridges they find over crevasses will be firmer and less likely to collapse under the weight of the Sno-Cats.

All this was true, but there were great advantages: the well-marked trail laid out by Hillary and his team and, always, the generous presence of Admiral George Dufek.

Vivian Fuchs and his men were a brave sight as they left the South Pole, flags flying and cheered on their way by the 18 Americans who were spending the winter there on IGY scientific studies. The temperature was an almost sultry minus 25°C, with the wind at 40 kilometres an hour, as the vehicles lined up to travel north, for the first time down the 140E meridian to Depot 700.

They left behind their huskies and Peter Mulgrew, who had stayed on to maintain radio links for Fuchs

Left and above: *A dramatic contrast — Hillary's caboose and Weasel, left, compared with Fuchs's larger Sno-Cat.*

until he departed. Peter and the dogs were flown out some days later, courtesy of Admiral Dufek.

I have one criticism here. Fuchs in both his messages and later in his written account, seems to take help from the Americans almost for granted; he gives no indication that he understood the very grave risks the Americans undertook every time they landed on the plateau.

Ed also implies this in his book when he writes that he was surprised when Fuchs asked to have the dogs flown out. Ed adds: 'By his determination to keep a fatherly eye on the whole proceedings Admiral Dufek had quite transformed the situation.'

For the first few days, the British bowled along quite well coming across the New Zealand dump, left when they had shed everything except essential fuel and food on that last dash to the Pole on the third day.

Then near disaster on 29 January, when Geoffrey Pratt, the expedition seismologist was found unconscious in his Sno-Cat with severe carbon monoxide poisoning, caused by his driving with windows closed against the cold. Exhaust fumes had leaked in.

Without oxygen to flush Pratt's system, Fuchs radioed George Dufek to ask for a Neptune to be flown down to evacuate him to McMurdo. Two Neptunes flew up — one flying buddy for the other — but found it too dangerous to land on the plateau's rough surface. They parachuted two bottles of oxygen and a doctor on the aircraft radioed how to administer medical treatment. Pratt, happily, soon recovered and continued.

One day later, *Wrack and Ruin*, George Lowe's Sno-Cat that had been plagued with mechanical troubles, finally came to a grinding halt and had to be abandoned. George transferred all his photographic gear — which was quite considerable — to Pratt's *Haywire*.

Now they were in the crevassed area that had so hindered Ed and it was necessary to proceed very cautiously, hindered by minor breakdowns by various vehicles, but guided by the cairned and flagged route that Ed had left through the dangerous region.

With some relief they broke clear after three days and on 7 February arrived at Depot 700 which had, in the meantime, been stocked with extra fuel as Fuchs had requested. They had, surprisingly, covered 830 kilometres in 15 days, keeping close to the 56 kilometres a day Fuchs had said he wanted to average, even though he had managed only 27 kilometres a day from South Ice to the Pole.

Later that day, Ed arrived from Scott Base in the Beaver, flown by John Claydon and accompanied by Derek Wright, who wanted desperately to get some film of Fuchs's progress for home consumption.

The weather had been very patchy, and John had taken six hours to fly up, detouring through unfamiliar mountain passes. John and Derek stayed almost 24 hours, waiting for the weather to clear before departing, and on 10 February Fuchs's party moved forward again.

Fuchs was, as usual, being very tight-lipped about his progress and down in McMurdo Sound none of us knew how the party was faring, although Derek was able to give me a first-hand account of what he saw. In fact, as we learned later, they were slowed considerably by constant bad weather, drifting snow and crevasses. More often than not, Ed was out in front on foot, feeling the way.

There was some light relief for the crossing party on 12 February, when they stopped for a maintenance day and Ed broke out a bottle of whisky he had brought up to celebrate Bunny Fuchs's 50th birthday the previous day. Typically, Ed said later that he was quite enjoying being an adviser instead of leader.

In London, the Savoy Hotel had obtained some good public relations out of this a week earlier by announcing they were flying a case of champagne and a large tin of caviar to Fuchs, trusting the services of British Overseas Airways Corporation, Tasman Empire Airways in New Zealand, a United States aircraft to fly the load to McMurdo and then the expedition's Otter aircraft to deliver the goodies to Fuchs on the plateau. Not unexpectedly, the gift never arrived.

On 17 February, the party reached Depot 480, the Beaver flew in again and we managed to get some news that was quite disturbing, as reported:

On foot, with a rope tied around his waist for safety, Sir Edmund Hillary led Dr Vivian Fuchs's Sno-Cats through 30 miles [48 km] of crevasses last Friday. For several hours he worked slowly forward in a blinding whiteout — caused by intense sunlight on the snow — while the Sno-Cats crept along behind him. All sense of distance was blotted out. Every yard of the way, Sir Edmund had to test the snow with an ice axe until he finally led the four vehicles to safety.

There were more mechanical delays, too. But also a welcome surprise: the trail the New Zealanders had left two months earlier was standing out clearly and was easy to follow: the Fergusons had compressed the snow under their tracks and because the surrounding snow was extremely dry it had just blown away, leaving the hard-packed trail standing up prominently.

On they pressed, with conditions little changed until 23 February when, as they neared the Polar Plateau Depot, the weather suddenly improved. For the first time in a month, they enjoyed a magnificent long sunset, and they were cheered to see Mount Feather in the distance marking where The Portal stood at the top of the Skelton Glacier.

Next day, they reached the Polar Plateau Depot where they stopped for a day to check supplies and were greeted by both the New Zealand Beaver and the British Otter, crowded with expedition members from Scott Base. There was a splendid feeling that the crossing was almost over.

But the long descent of the Skelton was still ahead and, as it turned out, visibility was so indifferent for most of the way that the Sno-Cats needed to follow a flagged route, set by Ed in the leading vehicle.

In spite of this, they were now on the home run and made good time, dropping from 2400 metres on the plateau to sea level at Skelton Depot in three days with — better still — the temperature rising from minus 35°C to around zero. They had moved from the onset of winter on the plateau to the last of a late summer on the Ross Ice Shelf. It was 28 February, and Scott Base was only four days of relatively easy driving away.

It was precisely 1.47 p.m. on 2 March 1958, when, with flags fluttering, Verey pistols firing coloured flares into the sky, an American band playing triumphal music and cameras clicking, that the four Sno-Cats trundled up the gentle rise leading to Scott Base and parked. In spite of all odds, the Commonwealth Trans-Antarctic Expedition had travelled 3440 kilometres in 99 days — almost exactly the time it had been planned to take, but one month late.

'It's wonderful to be here,' said Sir Vivian, ever low-key and just notified of the Queen's decision to knight him, as he swung down from his Sno-Cat, wearing the same black helmet, off-white turtleneck sweater and dark blue windbreaker that he had worn at the Pole.

'A piece of cake,' grinned Sir Edmund, in a khaki quilted anorak with the hood thrown back and goggles on his forehead.

The rest of the party joined them, shedding their windbreakers, scarves and caps, then stood about in the same clothing they had lived and slept in, with a brief break at the Pole, for 99 days. New Zealanders and Americans, almost all of whom would be wintering over, crowded into the mess room at Scott Base where there was a lot of beer and a huge welcoming cake with thick, coloured icing.

At the end of the trans-Antarctic flight, expedition crew members were greeted by Edmund Hillary. The story of their flight follows on page 154. From left to right: Flight Sergeant Peter Weston, Squadron Leader John Lewis, Sergeant Taffy Williams, Sir Edmund Hillary and Flight Lieutenant Gordon Haslop.

Sir Vivian disappeared almost immediately into the radio room where he was seen arranging to send several messages, then he reappeared with a huge sheaf of congratulatory telegrams, the first of hundreds that poured in during the next hours.

Sitting down with Ed Hillary to talk to clamouring journalists he said, in his rather formal way: 'Today is a great day. We are exhilarated to be here and with this reception.'

Did he ever think the expedition might fail?

'No, I don't think we ever despaired completely. But with the obstacles in the early stages, one wondered just how long one was going to take to overcome them.' He added: 'From Depot 700 on, Ed Hillary was with us and he was able to guide us. We missed crevassing only because Ed showed us the route. We broke only two crevasses after leaving Depot 700 and that was because I was off course.'

Both Fuchs and Hillary kept smiling broadly as they answered questions and it was made very clear that the controversy that had raged throughout the world before Fuchs reached the South Pole was not of their making, nor had they added fuel to it.

Ed claimed to create a record for driving a Sno-Cat while sitting backwards — this was when he drove the lead vehicle from the Plateau on to the Skelton in continual whiteouts while sighting flags set to the rear, at his suggestion, in order to keep a straight course. In one day 67 kilometres were covered this way.

He added: 'I think we got off the plateau just comfortably in time.'

Right: *A fine example of an hour-long sunset looking across to the western mountains from Scott Base.*
Below: *Journey's end for one of the New Zealanders' Ferguson tractors as it rests at the South Pole. The ring of oil drums can be seen above the bonnet. American scientists used the tractors for several years, ranging out from the Pole.*

Otter's flight

Almost without fanfare in the heat of the hellbent controversy, the four Royal Air Force members of the trans-Antarctic expedition flew their Otter aircraft from South Ice to Scott Base on 6 January 1958, completing the first single-engined flight across the Antarctic.

Squadron Leader John Lewis, Flight Lieutenant Gordon Haslop, a New Zealander, Flight Sergeant Peter Weston, the mechanic, and Sergeant Taffy Williams, the radio operator, took exactly 11 hours to fly 2288 kilometres, crossing directly over the South Pole station and making several tight circuits of the ring of oil drums marking the actual Pole before continuing down the

Beardmore Glacier, following the route of Scott.

We were all standing on the ice airstrip when they touched down at exactly 10.49 a.m. after being escorted across the Ross Ice Shelf by a fleet of American Otter and Dakota aircraft crammed with Americans and New Zealanders flourishing cameras.

The four RAF men had closed down Shackleton Base and then flown up roughly 480 kilometres to the deserted South Ice base to prepare for the crossing. Although their flight from South Ice to Scott Base had been without incident, an attempt of the flight four days earlier had to be called off after meeting bad weather when about four hours out.

THE EMPEROR PENGUINS' FAREWELL

A school of emperor penguins swam around *Endeavour*, surfacing like porpoises as members of the British contingent of the Commonwealth Trans-Antarctic Expedition, along with Hillary and Miller, crowded on board and the ship prepared to leave. It was the evening of 5 March 1958.

McMurdo Sound was freezing over and most of the New Zealanders and all the returning Americans had already left on American ships. The emperors had stopped for a last farewell before moving on to their breeding ground at Cape Crozier. Occasionally the emperors threw themselves up on to the edge of the bay ice, exploding as penguins do through the thin surface ice, to land on their feet. Well over a metre tall and weighing some 25 kilograms, these permanent Antarctic residents waddled solemnly around among the crew and expedition members as though inspecting their work.

It was a bitterly cold evening, a light wind was blowing and the temperature was around minus 25°C. The sea surface was slowly turning to ice around *Endeavour* as the last expedition members boarded. The departure was dangerously late in the season and the ship was leaving not a moment too soon.

Further off in McMurdo Sound the United States naval ice-breaker *Glacier* was hovering, ready to break up the freezing sea and give *Endeavour* a friendly escort out into the ocean, but anxious to depart as quickly as possible. Admiral Dufek, ever a friend in time of need, had delayed *Glacier*'s departure for this purpose.

Once clear of McMurdo, *Endeavour* was soon pitching and rolling in a heavy Ross Sea swell, as only she could. Twelve days later, she sailed triumphantly into Wellington to a tumultuous reception from crowds gathered around the harbour and on the wharves. Ships' sirens screamed and Royal New Zealand Air Force Vampire jets swooped overhead. The British supply ship *Magga Dan*, which had taken Fuchs's team to Shackleton 18 months earlier, was also in port and sailed out to escort *Endeavour*, crowded with some of the British men's families.

What I can only describe as a rapturous heroes' welcome continued around New Zealand for the next four weeks as expedition members took a well-earned holiday. There were state and civic receptions, luncheons and dinners by Antarctic and related societies, up and down the country.

Then, on 12 April, most of the British members sailed on the passenger ship *Rangitoto* for Southampton, arriving home on 12 May to an equally enthusiastic welcome. They boarded a specially chartered train and were rushed to London for a Government reception.

Three days after arriving at Southampton, the British expedition members were driven through cheering crowds lining the streets of London to Buckingham Palace, where Queen Elizabeth formally knighted Vivian Fuchs and presented expedition members with Polar Medals and clasps.

The last great Antarctic adventure was over.

A splendid 1.2-metre high emperor penguin guards Endeavour *on the sea ice at McMurdo Sound. These magnificent creatures, unlike other penguins, are virtual nomads, spending the summer months feeding at sea in preparation for the long winter which they spend in communal rookeries on the sea ice near land.*

INDEX

(Bold text denotes pages with images)